Endorsements

"Is your life in turmoil due to a wayward child? If you feel caught between a rock and a hard place, second-guessing your childrearing decisions or responses, you may find a soul mate and help in the pages of this book. Author Anita Estes journals with refreshing candor and honesty about her prodigal son offering suggestions to parents in similar circumstances."

~Brenda Nixon, M.A., author of the award-winning *The Birth to Five Book* (Revell), speaker, and host of *The Parent's Plate* radio show on Toginet Media.

"Anita Estes has penned a book of hope and direction for any parent who has a child going down the road of addiction. These are times when depending on God is paramount and they are times to listen to those who have walked this painful road before. Wherever you are on the journey of addiction with a friend or loved one, the words of this book will help guide the prayers of your heart... and give you hope!"

~Joel Sheets, Executive Director, Transformation Life Center

Author Biography

Anita Estes resides in upstate New York with her husband and son, along with April and Bella, her matching pets. She enjoys the beauty of nature in the Hudson Valley and loves to photograph it. Her professional career is teaching, but she is also an author and avid gardener. As an educator, she has been honored in *Who's Who of American Teachers* for 2000 and 2005.

Her desire is to help others know God better, achieve their potential in Him, and encourage them in their spiritual walk. She also desires to reach out and comfort the brokenhearted and hurting through her writing and ministry. Her work appears in several devotionals and compilations including *Upper Room, God Allows U-Turns, A Cup of Comfort Book of Prayer, Penned from the Heart and Deliver Me.* She is also the author of *When God Speaks—40 Days and Nights of His Promises* and *Transformed—Inspiring Stories of Freedom.* Visit her at www.anitaestes.com

Letters to God, on a Prodigal Son

Overcoming Addiction Through Prayer

Anita Estes

"But You, O Lord, are a shield for me, my glory and the One who lifts up my head. I cried to the Lord with my voice, And He heard me from His holy hill" (Psalm 3:3-5).

Letters to God, on a Prodigal Son
Overcoming Addiction Through Prayer
Anita Estes

Copyright 2011
ISBN 9780982651018

Published by Transformation House

Transformation House is dedicated to bringing you books that proclaim truth with compassion. Their goal is to encourage people, bring hope to the hopeless, and demonstrate the power of God through the written word.

Unless otherwise indicated quotations are from the New King James version of the Bible (NKJV).

Table of Contents

Acknowledgements

I would like to thank the members of Transformation Life Center for their help in rescuing my son from darkness and putting him on the path of life. I would also like to thank TLC for their encouragement in writing the book and bringing it to completion. I would also like to thank my daughter, Joanna, for her help with the graphics and my family for their patience as I work on my books. I would like to thank those who helped with editing the book and contributed ideas. I especially want to thank my prodigal son for listening to God and answering His call to come back home into the family of God.

Introduction

If you are in the midst of dealing with someone in your family who is caught in the grip of addiction, then I believe this book will minister to you. I have embarked on this mission in the hope that you will find comfort and healing in these pages. I trust my struggles and insights will help ease some of the pain and fear you are experiencing. I have opened a very personal window into my life, so you can know there is someone who understands your pain. My intention is to help guide you through the dangerous waters you will encounter—and find true hope. Let me assure you, this wasn't an easy journey with simple solutions. Nonetheless, the outcome was successful because of the reliability of the One I appealed to for help—the God of the universe and the maker of all life.

While everybody's story has its own unique features, I believe some common elements exist in which addiction develops and universal ways in which people deal with it— some more effective than others. This is not only the story of my son, but it is the heartfelt cry of a mother who sought God and found peace in the midst of a devastating experience.

The pain and sorrow of my son's addiction, taught me the value of Proverbs 3:5

(emphasis and parenthetical addition mine). *"Trust in the Lord with all your (my) heart, And lean not on your own understanding...."* This challenged me to put my trust in God even though the circumstances made no sense to me and I felt helpless. Yet in my weakness, I found God's strength was sufficient. May this story lead you into a greater understanding and trust in God and offer a lifeline of hope.

If you would like prayer for your prodigal, Please visit me at http://anitaestes7.blogspot.com

NOTES

The names of the individuals have been changed to protect their privacy.

All permissions have been granted for references to *The Worship Warrior* by Chuck D. Pierce and *The Sword of the Spirit, The Word of God* by Joy Lamb.

The *Sword of the Spirit* is available from Christian Healing Ministries, P.O. Box 9520 Jacksonville, Florida 32208 Fax # 1-904-765-4224

Anita Estes' books are available on Amazon and her website at www.anitaestes.com. For comments you can contact her at **anitawriter7@yahoo.com**

"Weeping may last for a night, but a shout of joy comes in the morning"(Psalm 30:5 NAS).

2006

Warning Signs
Financial Problems

Early September

I feel the earth trembling beneath my feet once again and I'm afraid. I thought our prodigal son, Ben, was back on solid ground, but I'm not sure now. He's having problems already.

Dear God,
I can't believe this is happening. Ben called in a panic from school and complained that he didn't have the proper attire. He got kicked out of class because he didn't have on the right kind of sneakers! He gave me a story and explained that he didn't have the money to buy them. Why not? I've got a gut feeling the problem may be deeper than this. I sure hope I'm wrong.
I'm on the train now going to New York City with the girls, and they're annoyed I took his call, but I had to understand the situation. Ben said he spent the money I gave him for food and rent. I thought I supplied enough to cover expenses, but he needed a month's deposit for the rental, which we hadn't taken into account.

9

That's possible, but is he telling the *whole* truth?

Ben wants me to find his bank branch and deposit $40.00 for the required footwear. The girls yelled at me because I told him I'd try to do it. I guess they're angry because so much of my time lately has been consumed by him, but I'm confused. If I don't help him out, he'll miss the first week of classes. The instructor told him he couldn't come back without white sneakers. How can I refuse such a small request?

My Lord, by the end of this conversation, I was the one in a panic. Ben sounded scared and wanted to come back home. Why does he get so easily derailed? I'm puzzled. He spent two years of his life preparing for this career, and now he wants to end it after the first few days of school. Why does he get himself into these situations? Is he still too immature at twenty-three to handle the responsibility?

Dear Lord, Please give me wisdom and show me what to do. Help Ben get his feet on the ground and get this degree!

<u>Lessons Learned</u>: Ben's panic and lack of money were warning signs of a deeper problem. Because I didn't know the root cause, I wanted to give him the benefit of the doubt and not jump to conclusions. I didn't know Ben wasn't really ready to handle a school over a thousand miles away. I wanted so much to believe he could do it. I knew he possessed the intelligence, but perhaps he didn't have the maturity. I thought he learned

his lesson years ago when he lent his college book money to a so-called friend who promised to give him back twice the amount. He never got the money so he went the semester without books and failed several courses. Ben came back home as a prodigal son and did better when he attended community college, so I thought he was ready to go back out on his own, but it was too big a leap for him. He wasn't well grounded yet and was too open to temptations and the suggestions of peers.

I believed in my son, so I gave him all the opportunities I could, but sometimes that isn't what's best.

Suggestions: When Ben was living at home, more open dialogue would have set the stage for a better understanding of his strengths and weaknesses. Even though he was more responsible at home, it didn't necessarily mean it would translate to going away to school, especially not one so far away. I believe it could have been better if we had waited longer until Ben proved that he could handle the responsibility of being away or attend a college closer to home. I think it's important for parents to understand the maturity level of their college bound child and what temptations they can and cannot handle. Also, I've been told by experts that addictions slow down or "freeze" the maturity level of the person at the age which they become addicted. So even though Ben was twenty-three, he acted like an eighteen year old.

Mid September
Dear Father,
        Benjamin keeps running out of money. He got the loan money and paid his bills, but then he lent a part of it to someone else for their rent because he felt sorry for them. I know Ben can be overly compassionate. You know he's done this before. How gullible. He thinks they're going to give him more money back becaue they say they would. Yeah right. He'll be lucky to see any of it. I don't know why he jeopardizes his own welfare to help others? Please help him to see that this loan money shouldn't be used for others. I think I might need to go down there and check up on our son. Several people agree, including my husband. Maybe I can find a good church down there he could connect with. Please give me wisdom to know what I should do.

Lessons Learned: These were further warning signs. Not only was Ben mismanaging his money, but he was gullible. He was willing to put himself at risk for the sake of others who took advantage of him. Because Ben didn't judge people accurately, he believed people who were not trustworthy. He wanted to be accepted by others and was willing to do things that were risky. Our wayward son was using poor judgment, probably because his thinking was clouded—more so than I knew.

12

<u>Suggestions</u>: Ben needed to be more accountable for his finances when he was at home and away. Written records of his spending needed to be instituted earlier in his life. Although I helped Ben with making a budget, the deeper issue was his vulnerability—lending money to please others. My husband and I needed to probe more and not allow this, even if Ben didn't like it.

In addition, Ben wasn't willing to talk about the reasons why he did things, so we didn't understand some of his issues. However, we could have explored other avenues in our communication to open him up more and probe further. I always thought of him as a "good boy" and trusted him.

However, when Ben was a teenager he received a DUI (driving under the influence) and went for only two counseling sessions, which alerted us that he didn't want to own up to his actions. The counselor said he was fine, but our son was being evasive and manipulative—two character traits of many people with addictions. Though I believe God worked things out in the long run, we could have helped Ben develop more responsible behavior. We could have required that he reap greater consequences for his negative actions.

Late September
Dear Father,
Benjamin called and is having greater

financial problems. I questioned him, and he finally admitted it. He's been smoking pot, and much worse. Here's the clincher—he tried cocaine! I nearly fell over and dropped the phone. Why in the world is he doing that? Doesn't he know how bad that is for him?

I've spent my whole life praying for this kid. Haven't you heard me, Lord? I can't believe You've let him fall so far from the truth God. We sent him to a Christian school, and he winds up doing drugs!

I knew he use to smoke marijuana, but hard drugs like cocaine! What's happening to him down there? He said he wouldn't do it again, but he always says that when he does something wrong. He was doing better when he was living at home and going to school. He straightened out as far as I knew. He wasn't drinking or smoking pot, at least not heavily. Now this? It makes no sense. This is no longer just a tremor, but a full sized earthquake!

Dear God, please intervene. I pray You will help him can get his feet back on the ground. I hope he doesn't throw away this opportunity.

<u>Lessons Learned</u>: Ben struggled to stop drinking and smoking pot whenever he was away from home. He did better when living at home and quit for months at a time, but my husband and I weren't aware that he had problems with addiction. Ben was good at covering things up. He never smoked pot or drank at home. Once I

found some white powder in his room, and my husband had it analyzed, but it turned out to be baking soda from chemistry class. I felt stupid for suspecting that it was cocaine.

Suggestions: Discussing issues and holding your prodigal accountable for their actions and whereabouts is very important. Since I didn't grow up around alcohol or drugs, I didn't know the warning signs: change of friends, depression, mood swings, financial problems, problems in school, lack of interest in previous pursuits, etc. On the other hand, when I talked to a drug and alcohol counselor regarding this, she said it's difficult when your child is an adolescent to determine the difference between normal teenage behavior as opposed to the beginning of an addiction. Though I feel I could have been more aware of what was beginning to develop in Ben's life, I'm glad I spent time in prayer, which I believe is one of the most powerful weapons we have against battling addictions and many other problems and issues.

Scriptures and Promises: During this time, fear and doubt haunted me. I continually talked to God and tried to hold on to some promises. My stomach flip-flopped, though I believed God could work on Ben and put him on the right path. These verses helped me from falling into despair:

- *"You will keep him in perfect peace whose*

15

mind is stayed on You, because he trusts in You" (Isaiah 26:3). This was a far cry from the actual situation, but I was learning, step by step, to trust God and believe He would eventually transform this terrible mess into something good.

- *"God works all things together for good for those who are called according to his purposes" (Romans 8:28)*. Though I wavered in this belief, I always came back to it. No matter what Ben went though, God could work it out for good. The problem was: would Ben allow God to work in his life? I hoped so.

- *"And my God shall supply all my needs according to his riches and glory" (Philippians 4:19)*. God's supplies are abundant, and I called upon Him day and night to get me through this emotional time and to keep me from getting really depressed.

- *"Trust in the Lord with all your heart and lean not unto your own understanding, in all your ways acknowledge him, and he will direct your paths" (Proverbs 3:5)*.This was one of my all time favorite verses, and it helped me to stay sane when I just didn't understand why Ben was making such a major mistake in his life.

16

Flirting with Addiction
A Rollercoaster of Emotions

Early October

Dear Father,

I feel as if I'm caught up in a tornado. I don't know how to get out. Everywhere I turn, there's a problem. Ben told me that he wasn't going to do drugs any more, but can I believe him? If we pull him out of school, we'll waste $20,000 dollars and three years heading towards this destination swallowed up in a snap! If we leave him there, the problem may get worse. What should we do Lord? Keep him there or pull him out? Even my husband, Holbrook, agrees that it's time for me to go down and see what's up.

I don't know where we went wrong. We sent him to a Christian school, raised him in a Christian home, and I stayed home to be with him instead of going to work. How did this happen? He told me he stopped smoking pot. Maybe he did for a while, but he always seems to start up again. I thought things were good with him before he left for Radiology school. This was such a great opportunity for him to get into the field he wanted. Maybe it was a mistake to send him down there, too many temptations. I hope this is just a little slip up, and he'll get back on track.

17

<u>Lessons Learned</u>: Ben admitted that his problem started in high school with drinking and smoking pot. He wanted to be accepted by others, and fit in with them. Actually, a few years ago when he returned from failing out of a state college, he admitted to trying some harder drugs like ecstasy. But he turned his life around, like a prodigal, and came back to the Lord. My husband and I believed he was back on a Christian path, and then the problem resurfaced. I hoped and prayed he would overcome, but I didn't know that would take a couple of years. I thought he would get back on the right track by finding a good church down there, but he wasn't ready yet.

<u>Suggestions</u>: Although Ben did well while staying at home, being far away put too many temptations in his path. I think it would have helped if we had waited until he was accepted to a college in the area, but I was impatient and jumped at this opportunity for Ben. I thought it was God's will, but I hadn't prayed about it enough. Don't be too quick to believe that every opportunity that comes to your children is one they should take. I can't stress enough the importance of prayer and waiting on the Lord for answers. But once again, God used this time in my son's life to show him how much he needed spiritual intervention.

18

Oct 12th

Dear Lord,

As Columbus embarked on the mission that opened up the New World, I'm setting off on my own mission to find the truth. I was torn about what to do, but You've given me peace about going. Thank You for helping me find the name of a church where we can go. I hope Benjamin will like it and go there on a steady basis. Maybe he just needs to get connected to the right people.

On my way to the airport I got a little lost and couldn't find the right way over the George Washington Bridge. Then a woman in an SUV, who I think was an angel in disguise, directed me. With hands griped to the steering wheel, I navigated between tractor-trailers, lights flashing messages for closed lanes, ramps exiting and cars coming out of nowhere. I flew over a sea of concrete and made it to the airport in NY. I'm learning to face my fears. What will I find when I come to Florida?

Please give me wisdom and discernment as I meet with my son. Show me what to do, what to say and what to pray. Help him be open to my suggestions and to listen.

Dear Father,

As soon as I landed, I met my first challenge. Ben's friends gave him wrong directions, and he missed the airport. Now he's back at his apartment and doesn't have enough gas to come and get me. Even though I was annoyed, I found a transporter van and I felt the Lord working things out. The woman driver had attended the church I wanted to take Benjamin to, and she said it was a good one. Imagine that. Out of all the people in Jacksonville, the Lord hooked me up with someone who knew that church. Maybe Ben is just a little lost. Maybe You can send him an angel to show him the way out of this.

Oct 13th

Dear Father,

It is so good to see my son. Thank you Lord; he seems to be doing well in school. He looks a little skinny, so I'll have to fill his cupboards. There's nothing in them. He's in classes now and I met his teachers. They say he's doing well. No sign of trouble. Maybe my fears have been unfounded. Maybe he's going to be okay. Thank You Lord.

Sunday we went to a great church. I introduced him to the both the regular and youth pastors. I hope he will connect there. I'm not thrilled about where he is staying. I think there may be some drugs around. The people at the apartment are a little strange. We met one woman who kept encouraging Benjamin to continue with school, but something didn't seem right with her. Later, Benjamin told me she had a cocaine problem. Boy was I naive! I thought she was just the nervous type. And to think I went to a college in a hippy town with pot all around. Now people are caught up in far worse drugs like crack and cocaine. Things have certainly gotten worse!

I might need to look for some other places for him to live, though he signed a lease. Please Lord, show me if he should break it. Help him to connect with other Christians and the people in the Radiology program. Keep him away from bad influences.

<u>Lessons Learned</u>: I wanted to believe Ben. He said he could make it there staying at that apartment complex, but I knew it would be a struggle if he didn't get it together with the Lord. Later he admitted he started smoking crack with the neighbor next door! At first he was horrified that she smoked crack, and wondered why she did it. But before too long, he found himself sucked into it.

I beat myself up over this for a while. I'd found other apartments in the area, and even called to get him in, but Ben wouldn't move. He didn't want to break the lease. I could have insisted, but I was trying to let go and let him see if he could do this on his own. It was one of the hardest things for me to do.

<u>Suggestions</u>: Sometimes you just have to let your prodigal fall if that's what they're bent on

doing! I could've insisted Ben move out of the apartment, but he was old enough, twenty-three, to make his own decisions, even if they were bad ones. He had to learn to live with the consequences. If I was permitted to give only one suggestion to parents (other than praying), it would be this—allow your children to experience consequences from a young age. Let life teach them the hard lessons they need to learn. Don't be too quick to intervene.

Oct 14th

I bought several books on spiritual warfare down here to give to Ben, and he's been reading them. Today I discussed some of the principles with him. I told him that the word for drugs come from the root word *pharmakeia,* which in Greek refers to sorcery and witchcraft. It is the root word for our modern English term pharmaceuticals. I explained that using drugs, even those considered less harmful, such as marijuana, was in fact related to sorcery. He somewhat agreed, and he told me he wasn't going to use drugs anymore. Ben also agreed with what the book said about different spirits that are in control over regions. He said he has seen demons before.

I remember when he came home several years ago, frightened to death about an encounter he told me about. He said a demon was after him and trying to kill him. He made a complete turnaround at the time, and I thought that was going to be the last of his drug days. At that time, he confessed to me the drugs he had experimented with—pot, ecstasy, and cocaine, but he said that was the end of it for him. He did pretty well for a couple of years, and I thought all was well, until now.

<u>Lessons Learned</u>: Ben stayed away from drugs for quite a while, but he slowly got back into drinking and smoking pot. I wasn't aware of this, as he never did these things at home. Since he was in his early twenties, going to school and working, I was trying to give him more freedom. He'd attend church once in a while, then he'd stop going again, and return to the same old friends. I think that both me and my husband, who had experienced some of these problems, could have done more to get Ben talking about his relapses and what it meant to truly be a Christian—how a relationship with God will help keep us stay away from temptations. I think discussing his inclination to use drugs and his father's past problems may have helped, but we couldn't force our son to communicate. Most of all, my husband and I needed to pray for Ben, which I did ever increasingly during this time.

Powerful Scriptures:

Ben was in a spiritually vulnerable place, and he needed to follow the antidote for this. Since he didn't seem to be in the place to do this, I needed to click into prayer warrior mode, and stand in the gap for him. The following scripture has always been one of my favorites when involved in spiritual warfare—that is wrestling in prayer against the forces of darkness. *"For we do not wrestle against flesh and blood, but against principalities, against powers, against the rulers of the darkness of this age, against spiritual hosts of wickedness in the heavenly places" (Ephesians 6:12).*

However, before doing this, it's important to daily put on the armor of God as explained in these verses: *"Finally, my brethren, be strong in the Lord and in the power of His might. Put on the whole armor of God that you may be able to stand against the wiles of the devil. Therefore, take up the whole armor of God that you may be able to withstand in the evil day, and having done all, to stand. Stand therefore, having girded your waist with truth, having put on the breastplate of righteousness, and having shod your feet with the preparation of the gospel of peace; above all, taking the shield of faith with which you will be able to quench all the fiery darts of the wicked one. And take the helmet of salvation, and the sword of the Spirit, which is the word of God; praying always with all prayer and supplication in the Spirit, being watchful to this end with all perseverance and supplication for all the saints" (Ephesians 6:11-18).*

I realized that Ben was up against the spirits of darkness, but I didn't know to what degree. I also didn't know at the time how much I

24

needed to put on my armor so that Satan wouldn't catch me off guard or get me so depressed I wouldn't pray or have faith. Prayer and believing God's Word were my greatest weapons against what was happening, and so I used it. (But I hadn't completely learned that lesson yet. The worst was yet to come. I was about to learn how to pray even more fervently for my prodigal son.)

Dear Father,

In the name of Jesus Christ, I come against the spirits of drug and alcohol addiction in Ben's life. I break the hold they have over our son. I come against the strongholds of deception and rebellion, as Ben is not following Your ways. Help him to see what he is doing. Lead him into truth. Bring him back to You and Your truth. Cover him with the blood of Jesus, watch over and protect him. In Jesus' name. Amen.

Oct 15th

Dear Lord,

The visit was good, but Benjamin learned some hard lessons. He discovered that his so-called friends cheated him out of his rent money. He's fallen again into a bad crowd. I don't understand why he does this Lord. Does he think so poorly of himself? Why can't he make friends with Christians? I pray he will. He's so easily

25

taken in by others. He signed up a friend for a cell phone, which I was concerned about. We went to the phone store, but they couldn't locate his account so maybe it will be okay. I hope Benjamin learns how to handle money and bills. We prayed a lot about a number of things, both spiritual and practical so I anticipate this will have a positive effect on him. I brought him a book about spiritual warfare, and he started reading it. Please help him to be committed to what he promised—that he won't do any more drugs, especially cocaine. I pray that was a one-time experience.

Lessons Learned: It may have helped to take Ben out of that environment, but he needed to learn how to use better judgment for himself. He was not able to resist living around drugs, but I wasn't aware of how prevalent it was at the time. I thought that his building was safe. It was quiet at night and no people hung around during the day. He told me the people next to him were in the military. Even though it wasn't the best place, it wasn't the worst either. Now that I've gone through this ordeal, I think God will use even this in Benjamin's life. I believe he will be able to minister to others who are easily led astray while trying to do what they think is good. I also think Ben realizes now not to put himself in the path of temptation. This is a hard lesson for all of us to learn.

Oct 22nd

Dear God,

I'm so mad at Benjamin. He isn't answering his phone. I hope he's going to school and doing what he should do. Maybe he has too much time on his hands. School only lasts till noon. Maybe he should get a job, so he can have his own money and will be more responsible if he has to earn it. I don't understand why he doesn't answer his phone. Please help me reach him.

<u>Lessons Learned</u>: After I contacted Ben, he told me he applied for a job and got one at a local grocery store. I was happy he would be making some money of his own. Little did I know that this job would put Ben in contact with drug users and dealers. If I had known that, I wouldn't have pushed him to work. Yet God in His mercy redeemed this situation, and I learned a valuable lesson—not to push my agenda.

I had to learn this lesson over and over again in this situation with my son. Pushing my plans on Ben to go to college in Florida hadn't exactly paid off either, but once again God was merciful. I asked Him to help me be less pushy and confessed my stupidity. He is always willing to forgive us when we mess up. The hard part is admitting it, but it feels great when we do. That's one of the great benefits of having a personal relationship with Jesus—you can confess your sins, and you don't need to feel guilty any more.

Self-Deception

November

Dear Father,

I called the church where Benjamin and I attended, but he only went there one other time. I thought he would get connected to them, but he didn't. Now he's in trouble again—without gas money. This is getting bad. He keeps telling me he lends it to friends. I hope and pray he isn't using it on drugs. The church is going to lend him $5.00 for gas so he can get to school. He's not allowed to miss more than 3 classes or he doesn't pass the semester. He told me he's only missed one class and was only five minutes late for another. I pray he is telling me the truth. In the morning when I look over at the rooster on the coffee cup I bought at the dollar store down there, it seems like it's crowing, "Wake up!" I feel like such a fool. I don't know what is really happening and what to do.

Lessons Learned: I wanted to believe my son, but he hadn't set a very good track record. I should have asked a lot more questions when I was there, but I saw a temporary change in him. He prayed with me and went to church. He wanted to do good, but he just didn't know God's definition of righteousness. Somewhere along the line he missed understanding this.

A Powerful Promise:

I quoted the following scripture often. It was one of my favorites, giving me hope for Ben's situation. *"For I know the thoughts that I think toward you, says the LORD, thoughts of peace and not of evil, to give you a future and a hope" (Jeremiah 29:11).* Just what I needed to hear. Yes, God would take care of it all. He had good plans. I prayed Ben would get though this and graduate. It was okay to hope for this, but I was closed minded. My thoughts and plans were not necessarily God's thoughts and plans, but I wasn't ready to see that at the time. I wanted to be hopeful and believe Ben would graduate. Still, God eventually did work everything out for good, but according to His timing, not mine.

End of November

Dear Father,

I've called Benjamin a hundred times, but I haven't heard from him. I'm praying night and day that he will pass his classes. He needs to take a drug test, and I hope he is staying clean. Please convict him, Lord. Help him to repent. He got a job so maybe he won't need money so often. He hasn't called as much in desperation, so maybe that's a good thing. I pray he will come to his senses and see he needs to get his act together. Ben's twenty-three now, and should finish college soon. If he gets though this program, he can get a good job. Maybe he'll stop hanging around with the wrong people. He said he wants to finish the program and that he's interested in it. I really want him to finish school. That's the tough part. I need to trust You that he'll get through this.

Lessons Learned: I was focusing on the wrong things. I wanted my son to pass the classes so much and finish school that I was blind to what was really happening. At the time, all I could see was Benjamin graduating, getting a good job, and getting on with his life. I prayed day and night for this. While it helped to give me hope, it put me in the driver's seat instead of God. I didn't really want to know God had other plans. I wanted everything to work out for good as I saw it.

Suggestions: Sometimes we (especially me) are too much in a hurry for our children to be successful and make it in life. If we look back on our own lives, we can often see that it took some real life situations to teach us what we now know. Of course, we want to help our children avoid some of the same pitfalls, but we can't force them to learn. I needed to trust God more and not press Ben so much. I think if I would have done that, I wouldn't have pushed Benjamin into situations he wasn't really ready to handle.

Perhaps if you step back and look at the whole state of affairs, without putting pressure on yourself and your child, you will have more wisdom for what you are facing.

Dec. 8th

Dearest Father,

These two months were some of the most difficult of my life. Benjamin put us through hell. He lost or wasted over $2,000 dollars. He got himself involved with the wrong crowd. Why does he always seem to do this? Though I went down in October, it doesn't seem to have made an impact. Why not? Is it just that he is stubborn, stupid or mentally ill? Why does he let people take advantage of him? He's fallen in with a bad crowd—again!

I am stricken. I feel like David when he was praying and fasting in sackcloth and ashes, begging You to heal his son who was deathly sick. David entreated the Lord, but the baby died. I feel as if Benjamin has died. I don't think he'll pass this drug test, though I haven't found out for sure.

I felt it was You who woke up me in the middle of the night to pray for him. I spent the night wrestling with the fact that he probably has thrown this opportunity away. Now I am faced with the possibility that he might have a drug addiction. I have never prayed so fervently in all my life. Dear God, please deliver my prodigal son and have mercy on him. Protect Ben, and keep him away from drugs. Help him to pass his courses. However, if he needs to pay the consequences for his actions, and be kicked out of school—so be it, but I really want him to make it through this.

How my heart fails me. Replace these fears of mine with your peace so that I will be able to declare as the psalmist did, *"The Lord gives and the Lord takes away, blessed be the name of the Lord" (Job 1:21).* May I come to that place. I'm not there yet.

Life Giving Scriptures that Helped me Hang In:

This was a hairy time for me. I felt like a cat dangling in the air, while hanging onto a limb with one claw. I was afraid to let go, and let God, but these verses eased my burdened heart.

"If God be for us (I substituted me) who can be against us?" (Romans 8:31—parenthtical material mine). I believed God was on our family's side and that we would eventually win this battle together. I just wasn't sure how it would be resolved.

"God is my refuge and strength, a very present help in trouble. Therefore we will not fear, Even though the earth be removed, And though the mountains be carried into the midst of the sea" (Psalm 46:1-2). I drew on this verse for God's strength. I tried not to be afraid, but I had a lot to fear for Ben. I tried to steel myself against the inevitable. My son was going to fail

the drug test and be kicked out of the program. Even if this were so, the world would still be intact. I certainly would be shaken, though it wasn't what I wanted to happen. I thought Ben would come home and get into a drug program, but then something surprising happened.

Suggestions: Find some scriptures and promises of your own that ring true to you and your situation. Write them down, memorize them and quote them frequently when doubt and fear overwhelm you. Perhaps some of the above mentioned verses ministered to you. Feel free to highlight or copy any verses that help you, but make them your own. Ask God to give you wisdom what verses apply.

False Hope

December 10th

Dear Father,

Benjamin called me and told me he hasn't done any hard drugs in a while. What's a while? He assured me he'd pass the drug test. But doesn't he see the larger issue? Any drugs at all are a problem. Why does he do them in the first place? Did we do something wrong? Does he have a mental problem? Is he looking for acceptance with his friends? Show him the central issue he needs to deal with that causes this negative behavior.

Lessons Learned: Many questions plagued me; I wanted to understand why Ben did drugs. I thought it had to do with being accepted by others, and perhaps being depressed. Two years later my son acknowledged that both of these factors were true. Depression ran in the family. Ben admitted that when he was nineteen, he went into a deep depression when he went away to college. He didn't show it a lot, though we did try to get him to go to a counselor on a regular basis, but he refused. True to form, he only went a few times, and then he said he was fine. What we didn't realize at the time was that he tended towards addictive behavior and the addictive personality. My husband had struggled with drugs and alcohol, but overcame them when he became a Christian. We should have been more alert to the signs of depression and done something about it, but it was difficult when Ben was away at college most of the time.

December 12th
    Alleluia!!! Praise the Lord. God performed a miracle. He was faithful. He heard my prayer! Benjamin passed the drug test and all his courses. He is coming home for Christmas. God heard the cry of my heart and allayed my fears. Your name is greatly to be praised!

<u>Lessons Learned:</u> Though I was very concerned, I should have realized that Ben's passing the drug test was only temporary, but at the time I needed some victories to hold unto. I used this success to put into practice another strategy—praise. I had something to praise the Lord about, and I wanted to give Him honor. (The upcoming months would teach me to thank and praise Him, even when the situation looked bleak).

Praise and Promise Scriptures:
    I wanted to give praise to the Lord that Ben passed his first semester in the Radiology program. I was thankful that he heard my prayers. *"O Lord, O Lord, How excellent is your name in all the earth, Who have set your glory above the heavens! What is man that you are mindful of him?" (Psalm 8:1& 4).* I felt humbled

35

that God answered my heart cry.

"My God shall supply all our needs according to His riches and glory" (Philippians 4:19). This verse was an oldie, but a goodie. I quoted it often, almost every day. I felt God had supplied our needs; Ben was safe. He passed the drug test and the semester in good standing with a 3.0. God supplied out of the riches of His mercy.

Dec.23rd

Dearest Father,

Thank You so much. Benjamin seems to be doing well. This is my best Christmas present, seeing him talking and interacting with others, acting normal. Maybe he has overcome. Maybe my son doesn't have a drug problem, but just flirted with drugs. I hope so. This is the best Christmas I've experienced in a while. I love having all my family and children here with me. Thank You very much.

Lessons Learned: God allowed a respite in the situation. His mercy flowed over Ben, but he only temporarily showered in it. He could have turned completely away from his problems if he was honest with himself and turned to God. Our prodigal was trying to play both sides—to do what he wanted and call himself a Christian.

Two years later Ben explained that he didn't understand this was outright sin and rebellion. He saw that other Christians did drugs, so what was wrong with it? Unfortunately, Ben had to fall further before he was willing to admit he had a problem.

<u>Suggestions</u>: Don't be too quick to believe that your adult or teenage child is telling you the truth, and the situation isn't as severe as you think it may be. Addictions usually follow cycles of ups and downs, which can fool us into thinking they are doing better. It is best to be conservative when assessing progress. In these instances, actions most definitely speak louder than words. Let them truly prove they have changed. Don't believe what they say. Addicts are very good at manipulating situations in their favor, especially with family members, so be cautious.

Dec. 28th

Dear God,
        I'm not sure what to think. Benjamin couldn't get up last night. We were going to take him to the city, but he admitted he had a little too much to drink the night before. At least he didn't do any drugs, but it still concerns me. That was his problem when he failed out of the other college. He said he wasn't interested in the engineering program, but he even failed out

when he changed majors. I hope this is not going to be a recurring problem. Give me wisdom, Lord. Perhaps I should take him to a Christian counselor. I'll make the appointment and hopefully he will go.

Dec. 29th

Dear Father,

Thank You Lord. Benjamin went to the counselor. Ben took his phone number and said he would stay in contact with him. The session went well. I stayed in for part of it. I think he'll be okay. Please help him to stay on the right track. I just hope he stays away from poor influences and from drugs.

Lessons Learned: Although the session went well, I should have seen the crack in Ben's armor, but I didn't realize it at the time. He disagreed with the counselor about not drinking at all. Ben didn't see his own weakness at the time. He thought a few beers were okay, which for many people it is, but not for him. He didn't understand that alcohol was the beginning of his problem, but neither did we. He was the type that drank one beer, and it led to another and then other drugs, though it was a slow progression over time. I learned this is true for many alcoholics and drug addicts, but it would be a lesson my prodigal wouldn't learn for a few more years.

2007

Winter

January

Dear Lord,

Benjamin is back in school. He's doing his internship and driving to school everyday. I hope drinking doesn't become an issue. I'm so worried, God. I hope he can stick to his promises; I pray he wants to stick to them. Please help him to stay away from the wrong people. Today he found out that the guy he signed up for a cell phone never paid any bills for months, so Benjamin is responsible for it—over $500. Lord, will this ever end? When will he not be so gullible? Why does he do these things?

January 10th

Ben called and told me he was having problems with his car. He walked to the hospital where he's doing the internship, which was a couple of miles. He was upset because they only allow them to be late once. They said he couldn't be late again, even if he did have to walk two miles. He seemed discouraged.

Dear Lord,

I don't know if Ben can handle this. Things don't seem right. Why can't he get it together and do what he needs to do for school? There's always one problem or another. Now I haven't heard from him for a week, and he's not returning my calls. Something is not right. Father, please watch over and protect him. *"Give your angels charge over him, to guard him in all his ways" (Psalm 91:11).* Keep his Guardian angel close by his side.

Maybe Ben's just busy with the internship. The other day I saw his friend's mother, and she said she doesn't hear from her son for weeks. Ben's probably okay. I shouldn't worry so much. Please help me to trust You more.

Lessons Learned: I didn't realize Ben was falling deeper into addiction. Because of his condition, I was about to embark on a new venture of learning how to pray with all my heart and soul. At first, I agonized over Ben in prayer—heart sick with fear. This was interspersed with moments of faith when I claimed the promises from the Bible that were appropriate. Little by little my faith began to grow. Then later in 2007, I began to praise and worship the Lord through some of the darkest times of Ben's life.

Suggestions: It is difficult not to be consumed with your addicted child, but you must not put him or her first. Your marriage and your own physical, emotional and mental stability are very important in order to be able to see things from a clear perspective. While you can pray fervently, don't let the child or problem consume your thoughts and your time. Make time for you and your spouse, your other children and yourself. Spend time in prayer for other's needs as well as your own.

Life Changing Promises:

During this time I really learned how to pray the scriptures and promises. I needed encouragement everyday and some promises that I could hold onto continually. Here are two more that I clung to:

"God is our refuge and strength, an ever-present help in trouble. Therefore we will not fear, though the earth give way and the mountains fall into the heart of the sea, though its waters roar and foam and the mountains quake with their surging" (Psalm 46: 1-3 NIV).

Ben was certainly in trouble. I felt it. I knew it deep down in my soul—a gut feeling as some say. But at the same time, if I was going to stand in the gap for him and pray, I couldn't let this drown me. I certainly needed the reassurance that no matter what happened in the situation, if the ground caved in under me, God would still be there. And He was...even when the earth trembled and shook beneath my feet.

"Blessed be the Lord who daily loads us with benefits. The God of our salvation" (Psalm 68:19). Despite the circumstances, I worked on

41

believing God's Word over my own feelings. We were a Christian family who believed God was able to save. He would bless us, one way or another. I held onto the belief that Benjamin would return to the God of his childhood and salvation.

End of January

Dear God,

You know how worried I've been, well things are as bad as I imagined...even worse! Benjamin finally called tonight after I hadn't heard from him in weeks. I can't get straight answers from him. Who in the world is he involved with? A group of guys wouldn't give his car back. He finally told them he would call the police, and they gave it to him. He said he feared for his life. Dear Lord, this is terrible news. I knew something was wrong. Father, I beg you once again to *"Surround him with your angels, put them in charge of him and keep him safe" (Psalm 91:11).* Please don't let him get hurt and keep him away from evil.

What kind of people is he associating with? I'm so worried for him. I don't understand why he does these things. Why is he hanging around with people like this? What should I do?

Lessons Learned: That evening, the earth as I had known it slipped out from under me. It was one of the darkest hours of my life, followed by many restless nights. Ben admitted to me months later that he allowed drug dealers to use his car, and they were annoyed with him when he wanted the car back. He gave them a key, which they wouldn't give back to him. He was afraid they would steal his car from him, but more so he feared for his life! He hinted at this over the phone and it ignited my prayer life as no other realization ever had. During this time I prayed with much intensity, like only a mother can pray.

Later Ben told me the whole story, which was even worse. He moved out of his apartment with the drug dealers, and was sleeping in a roach infested apartment so they could use his car whenever they wanted to in exchange for drugs! I thank God that the Lord lit a fire under my prayers and brought me into a whole new realm of spiritual warfare. He also showed me an important principle of standing in faith. My prayers, which started out as agonizing over the situation, turned to prayers of victory, once I caught hold of God's power and ability to free Ben from whatever kept him bound.

Dear Father,

Thank You Lord that I just found a paperback on my bookshelf about praying Your Word—*The Sword of the Spirit, The Word of God* by Joy Lamb. It uses the scriptures for

43

praying about particular situations. God, you know Benjamin is getting worse, but the book says to thank You before I actually see the situation turning around...to pray like this: I thank You Lord, *"That the eyes of those who see will not be blinded, and the ears of those who listen will hear" (Isaiah 32:3).* My son once knew You and loved You. Open his eyes again. Help Benjamin to see what he is doing. He is not acting rationally. I don't understand why he is putting his schooling in jeopardy. Help him to get through this and keep him safe.

Thank You Lord that *"You will protect him from all evil; You will keep His soul" (Psalm 127:7).* In Jesus' name. Amen.

Death of a Dream

Beginning of February

Dear God,

Something's wrong. Terribly wrong! I can feel it. You awoke me up in the middle of the night. Why? My heart is racing. Is Ben in trouble? Is he in mortal danger? Please watch over him and protect him. The sound of his voice last evening was very disturbing. He's in deeper trouble then he wants me to know. Dear God, help me to believe, *"No weapon formed against him will prosper" (Isaiah 54:17).* Even though Satan is trying to destroy him, You will protect him from all harm. Thank you Father, Thank You for Your protection. In Jesus' name. Amen.

Last night the Lord woke me up and I prayed for an hour. Today I went on-line and found a prayer ministry in Jacksonville, Florida. It's not just a fluke that Benjamin is in that very city. It's also another divine coincidence that it's one of the ministries of Joy Lamb, the author who wrote the book I found! I entered a number of prayer requests for Ben. First on the list was that he would wake up, come back to God and repent, and another prayer was that he would overcome his addictions.

Lessons Learned: *The Sword of the Spirit* by Joy Lamb would prove to be key in helping me to

45

overcome my fears, and in praying and claiming the promises. All the prayers and promises were preceded by "I thank You Lord." This was a bold proclamation that God had already heard and answered my prayers. Every morning, I began to recite five to ten verses that applied to Ben's situation. I memorized them and prayed them on the way to and from work. I said them before bedtime. I cried out to God when my heart felt like it was being ripped out of me.

Suggestions: To keep focused on the Word of God and His promises, read books that help you grow in your faith. Underline the key ideas and return to them when you are feeling weak. Either post scriptures in your house to encourage family members, or write them down on index cards and have them readily available when needed. Plan for the times you will feel discouraged, and have a strategy for overcoming negative thinking: read a scripture, call a friend or put on praise music.

Dear God,

Only You know what plagues Ben. Only You know why he does the things he does. Please help him. Keep him safe. Thank You Lord that "*You will protect (Ben) from trouble and surround him with songs of deliverance" (Psalm 32:7)*. You will be his deliverer and get him out of this bad situation. Help him to do what is right. Watch over him, and cause him to turn his life around. Thank You Lord that Benjamin will *"Repent and turn to God performing deeds appropriate to repentance" (Acts 26:20).*

<u>Lessons Learned</u>: These verses became two of the promises I claimed on a daily basis. Whenever my faith wavered and I became fearful, I would hold unto these promises. I knew Ben repented a number of times before, but he kept slipping back each time, further and further away from the truth. Now I understand why he fell back. He didn't understand how to live righteously, because he wanted to do things his way. So I prayed daily, sometimes hourly—believing that when he repented this time, he would walk the talk. Two years later, I saw these two promises fulfilled.

<u>Suggestions</u>: Repentance is a key factor in dealing with addictions. Pray that God will soften the heart of the person with the addiction—that their eyes will be opened to see what they are doing and will be willing to change. However, you need to be sensitive to the person with the addiction. Be honest, but don't hit them over the head with the Bible and the Word of God. Use it as a secret weapon!

Feb. 10th
I'm a nervous wreck. I don't know what to do. Lord, help me to trust that You are at work in his life. I've been calling Ben everyday waking

him up for school. He's back in his apartment, and he said everything's okay. What a fiasco! He lent the apartment out to someone else who said they'd pay the rent, but they didn't. Benjamin didn't have the money for the rent, so he lived with friends. I said I would pay the rent, but I don't know why he can't budget his money right. What is wrong? Now he's back in the apartment, but he still doesn't sound right.

Suggestions: Even though I began to trust God more, there is nothing wrong with fervent prayer that rises from the depth of your soul and cries out to God for mercy. Just read the Psalms. Don't think you have to be calm and all together when you approach God. He understands the deep pain you are going through. He watched his only begotten son agonize at the Garden of Gethsemane and on Calvary to save his sons and daughters—for you and me and your addicted child, brother, sister, friend or relative. Let God know your heart.

Dear Father,

Please minister to Benjamin. Something is obviously wrong. Why does he make such poor decisions? He thought he could save money by subleasing his apartment and not have his own place to stay. That makes no sense. Help him to see what he is doing wrong. Cause him to repent. Thank You Lord that someday *"He will walk in the way of good men, and keep the path of the righteous"* *(Proverbs 2:20).* He will walk according to Your Word, and not according to his own thinking.

<u>Lessons Learned</u>: I claimed this promise daily and believed Ben would eventually come to this place, but at the time he wasn't ready. Benjamin was trying to do things his own way. He wasn't thinking rationally. He'd give money away then not have enough for himself. He possessed poor judgment because he was using drugs, and because Satan deluded him. Ben opened himself up to all kinds of wrong thinking by getting involved with drugs. It would take a while before my son understood or recognized this. In the meantime, I kept on praying.

Feb. 12th

I couldn't get a hold of Benjamin for a few days, so I called the school. My heart was palpitating as I talked to the director. She told me the ugly truth. Benjamin was no longer in the program. Dead air filled the phone lines. It felt like someone put a bullet through my heart. All the years wasted preparing for this, not to mention $20,000 in school loans down the drain. What are we going to do now? God, I feel You abandoned us, although I know that's not true. Benjamin has his own will, and he certainly has been exercising it. What do we do now?

Dear Jesus,

Help! I can't believe Benjamin let his schooling go down the tubes. Why is he acting so irrationally? He was a bright boy when he was younger. I don't understand why he's chosen this path of drugs. Is he really a drug addict or does he just have a problem with drugs? Whichever Lord, he needs Your help. I think his problem stems from the mental illness in our family line, the depression on both sides of the family and the bipolar disorder. Years ago, his father experienced problems with drugs, so now it's being passed on. Why? Please turn this around. Don't You hear my prayers anymore? Thank You Lord that You will *"Turn this curse of addiction into a blessing for us because you love us"* *(Deuteronomy 23:5)*. You do love us, don't You Lord?

Lessons Learned: I grappled with whether a loving God could allow this to happen to our son. I didn't understand why God let Ben go. I felt that my husband and I did everything we could to raise him as a Christian. Sure, we made mistakes, but we always tried to love him and guide him to God. At times, I felt somewhat abandoned by God, though I still prayed. What I didn't understand at the time was that God did not let go of Ben; Ben had let go of God.

Suggestions: Don't give up hope, even if the

50

circumstances worsen. Keep praying, keep believing. I've known people who were addicted for years, then turned from their ways and came to the Lord. Most people who have broken free from addiction knew someone who was praying for them. <u>Be that someone</u>, no matter what.

Feb. 13th

Benjamin has not contacted us, so I phoned the pastor from the church. I asked him to visit our son and get back to me. I'm waiting to hear back from him. I feel in limbo, suspended between life and death, heaven and hell. I never thought I would raise a son who had a drug problem or worse yet, an addiction. This is almost too much to bear. What have we done wrong?

Dear Lord,

Heal this broken heart of mine. I come to You once again filled with the anxiety of raising a wayward son who has gone astray. Lord speak. I need to know Your mind in this. Mine is clouded and confused. I hear Your voice telling me *"Be still, and know that I am God" (Psalm 46:10)*. Lord I know you're there in the heavenlies, ruling up there, but down here on earth it's a mess. I'm groping to find my way though this dark night.

My heart breaks for the son I once adored. What's wrong with him Lord? He once loved You, but now he's lost. Bring him back home to You. Thank You Lord that You will *"Look upon his affliction and trouble, and forgive all his sins" (Psalm 25:18).* He's afflicted—a curse of genetics and/or Satan. Whichever, please Father, forgive him for he doesn't know what he's doing (paraphrase of Luke 23:34). Bring him home where he can find You again, forever and ever. Let it be so. Amen.

Lessons Learned: This was a very painful time for me. I tried to see things from God's perspective and have faith, but then I'd lapse into blaming everyone for Ben's problems: myself, my husband, our family gene pool, Ben's stupidity and even God at times. Yet in these months I cried out to God more and more. Even though this wasn't the end of my son's problems, it was the end of myself—my pride, self-reliance, judgmental attitudes and self-righteousness. And so, though it was the worst of times, it was also the best of times. It was the beginning of my awakening to the reality of Ben's drug addiction, and my helplessness without God's intervention.

Later that day

So many things have transpired in six hours. I have two opposing choices to consider. The pastor from the church visited Ben and called back. They said he should go home and check into a rehab. Ben is totally out of the Radiology program. He's talked about staying there and doing Forensics instead. Should he?

I felt the Lord urge me to go for a walk and think things over. It's an icy, windy day, not blustery like the Winnie the Pooh story we use to read together, but cold with snow in the forecast. The clouds partly obscure the sun. I feel this represents my life. I can't quite see what to do, and it's a cold, bleak time in our lives. I am looking for wisdom, for answers. I'm trying to listen to God's voice. What should we do? Should Ben stay or come home? Will he be able to go to school for another program or will he sink even lower?

Dear Father,

Thank You Lord that You have heard the cry of my heart, for You spoke to me in Your Word through Ecclesiastes 3:1: *"There is a time and a season for everything under heaven."* Now is the time for me to mourn. I pray You will take this ugliness, this sin in my son's life and transform it into beauty—if only Benjamin is willing. Let him call upon you this day. Thank You Lord that *"a sword will pierce his soul to the end that the thoughts from his heart will be revealed" (Psalm 51:10).* This is difficult for me to pray Lord, but show him where he has gone astray. Let him find his way to you, Oh Lord.

Father, forgive me for anything that I did in his life to cause this. He was so sensitive. I tried to understand, but I lost my temper sometimes raising three children. Please forgive me for sins known and unknown. Take this broken heart of mine; heal it one piece at a time. You have given me a difficult load to bear. First, I dealt with these problems with my husband, now my son. I can't leave him down there to get in a worse mess, so I'm going to buy an airplane ticket and go down there and get him.

<u>Lessons Learned</u>: I was so afraid of Ben sinking lower that I would do most anything to prevent it. I feared how low he would go. I didn't understand his addiction, but I was learning. His problem was a little different than others and he fooled me. He would walk the narrow road for a while and do better. I mistook this for being healed and completely clean, but he never stayed that way for more than six months. He had to see this lifestyle through to the end, and I needed to let him fall flat on his face.

Feb. 14th
Dear Lord,

I read in my daily devotional that when we go though times of darkness, it is a time for us to listen. I'm listening Lord! Speak to me. It's a wintry mix outside—snow and rain, with hail adding to the danger. The gentle falling snow has given way to sleet and freezing rain. Snow and sleet make for very dangerous driving conditions.

Ben is a wintry mix of snow and sleet. He said it himself. His flesh is stronger than his spirit. He wants to do good, like his own father, but it's difficult for him. He's driving down a dangerous path of addiction. I can hardly believe this is true. I should have opened my eyes wider, observed more.

If I put everything together that I've read in the last few days, it seems that You are saying that there is a time for judgment over Ben's actions and decisions. The book of Jeremiah shows this clearly. You gave the Israelites many chances, just as we gave Ben. God spoke to His people through Jeremiah that He would judge the nation, but they refused to listen. Judgment came though King Nebuchadnezzar. Benjamin has been weighed and found lacking. However, unlike the Old Testament, he doesn't need to be destroyed. Perhaps You'll put him in exile for a while, the way you did with the Israelites, then bring him back to You. But now it appears, this is a time of judgment.

The Bible makes it clear. *"God cannot be mocked. A man reaps what he sows" (Galatians 6:7).* Ben has sown some bad seeds, and he needs to reap the consequences without me stepping in and sheltering him. He needs to find these things out for himself. We gave him many chances and he's failed. I don't want him to see himself as a failure, but he needs to understand there are consequences to his actions. He's turned off his phone, avoiding us. He doesn't want to confront the issues and talk with us. What should he do? Almost everyone I spoke with thinks he should come home. Lord, what is Your will?

An Epiphany Isn't Enough

Feb. 16th

Dear Lord,

Ben called me while I was driving to work, and said he experienced a change of heart. He wants to come home! He said he would explain later, but he told me the oddest thing. He wants to come home so he can eat chicken nuggets in his own living room. I realize this represents the comfort and security of home. It's a small thing, but I'll take it Lord. He wants me to buy him a plane ticket for today! My goodness, how he lives his life on the edge, always in an emergency. But thank You that he came to his senses and wants to get out of there. I wish it hadn't come to this, but at least he's coming home.

A few hours later

He just called again in a panic, fearing for his life! He went to the apartment and packed for his flight. He wasn't able to contact his roommate, who didn't pay the rent anyway, so Ben packed up his things and left them outside. Just as he was leaving the roommate came back and went nuts. He punched the walls and toppled the refrigerator. Ben ran to the super of the complex, but they said it was his problem. Lord, protect him. Surround him with Your angels.

56

I called the church for him, and they're going to drive him to the airport. Thank You Lord that the roommate didn't hurt Ben. Perhaps he exaggerated. I hope the guy didn't do too much damage to the apartment and that Ben will not be held responsible it. What kind of person had he lived with? Anyway, Ben will be home this evening. I'm going to meet him at the airport. Lord, we'll have to take this one step at a time.

<u>Lessons Learned</u>: Ben wanted to come home and promised to change, so we accepted him back. Who knows what would have happened to him if he remained? He could have been hurt or killed if he stayed any longer in that city. While it hurt me that Ben came home from college again as a failure, at least he came home. I've known women who've lost their sons to drugs and alcohol or even a senseless accident. Life is fragile and I was learning to handle it with prayer. I was thankful for what came my way— even when it wasn't exactly what I wanted.

<u>Suggestions</u>: There is a time to let your adult child fall and a time to help them. The only way to tell the difference is to apply wisdom through prayer. It's important to weigh whether helping them will further their addictive lifestyle. You need to create a workable plan and make your prodigal accountable to someone reliable. He or she must be willing to change and put that into

action. Don't believe just talk.

February 17th

Dear Lord,

Today Ben told me he had an epiphany, and realized he had been doing wrong. He's experienced several of these before, but he said this time it was different. I agree; but I realize in order to make his resolutions stick, we need to require more of him. Holbrook and I will need to dish out some tough love with those chicken nuggets. Here's our plan:

- Give him a lot of praise for good decisions and a job well done, but require more of him.
- Curfews to be adhered to and honesty about where he's going.
- No staying overnight at a friend's house.
- Discuss heart issues and a plan to overcome problem areas.
- Help doing chores and pay rent once he gets a job.
- Spend bonding time with his father doing manly things like bringing in the wood.
- Some type of counseling or outpatient drug treatment program, dependant on recommendations of a professional.

Lessons Learned: My husband and I were trying to get Ben to change by putting restrictions on him. While we had the right to impose rules since he was living in our house, this plan wasn't going to change him until he was willing to admit he was wrong. Ben had an epiphany of sorts. He knew what he was doing was wrong and wanted to change, but he wasn't quite ready to completely quit following his own heart and mind. He hadn't resolved to do things God's way yet, though he was getting closer. We were getting on the right track too, but not quite there yet. It was a journey and learning experience for all of us involved.

February 18th

Dear Jesus,

My emotions have been all over the place, up and down like a roller coaster. I'm happy to see Ben and thankful that he is home safe and sound. At the same time, I'm angry he blew this opportunity, annoyed he wasted a lot of money yet again, and confused as to whether he has a minor problem with drugs or an addiction.

I'm frustrated with my husband for not being there for Ben when he was a teenager. I'm confused about how to deal with Ben, what to do with him and my emotions. Oh God, what is your will?

Thank You for the book I'm reading that seems to parallel what we're going through. Through all the difficulties and questioning, we can rely on God. He will show us the way, where there seems to be none. Love will tear down the walls between my husband, Ben and me. I pray Your love will build a bridge to understanding and resolution to these problems. Show us the way, O Lord. Guide us. Thank You that the *"Holy Spirit will lead us into all truth" (John 16:13)*, and that You will *"Sanctify them (Ben) in the truth. Your word is truth" (John 17:17— parenthetical addition mine)*.

February 26th
 I've been reading a lot in the Psalms. They are a comfort and a source of encouragement. Here is my own psalm.

A Psalm for Parents of Prodigals

Oh God, You are my God
         And I will worship You.
Though darkness and confusion
         engulfs me,
You will light my path.

Though heartache and disappointments
         Surround me,
You will lift up my soul.

You will meet me in my times of sorrow,
         And comfort me.
You will lead me and guide me
         when I don't know which way
                  to turn.

60

Though no one else may know the way,
    You will reveal it to me.
Though our enemy desires my son's life,
    You have spared him.

May he dedicate his life to You,
    And follow Your footsteps.
May You illuminate my son's path
      back to You, that he may walk
        Righteously in Your ways.
May You open my prodigal son's eyes
      for the task he is to do
        with his life.

Lord, look down upon us and lift us up.
      Thank You for preserving our life.
May You give us wisdom,
    And guide us in all we say and do.
I place my son and my husband
      in Your hands.
Soften their hearts towards You,
    And keep them moldable.
Let all of us be clay in Your hands. Amen.

Feb. 28th

    Benjamin's been home now for a couple of days, and I've been watching for signs of withdrawal, but I see none. He's sleeping a little bit more, but after all he's been though, that's to be expected. He doesn't believe he needs a drug rehab, though I would like him to go for at least a month. I called the Christian based center in this area, and they have a six-month minimum treatment program. Ben won't agree to that, and I'm not sure he needs it. However, I've contacted them and spoke with a young man who's from Florida, Jacksonville to be exact, where Ben just came from. He too came from a good Christian family, but got waylaid by drugs—meth to be exact. What is it about these boys? So many prodigals! Is Satan prowling about looking for who he can destroy, or is there another problem?

Lord, I wish my stubborn son would go for an interview at the rehab or at least talk to the guys. I've been watching Ben and talking to him a lot. I don't know what to think. He seems okay. He agreed to go to a counselor, so we'll see what he has to say about treatment.

Lessons Learned: Ben didn't realize back then he needed to go to a rehab, more for his spirit than for the actual addiction. He didn't understand that drugs and alcohol became his coping mechanism. He also didn't think he had a major problem. He thought it was under control. Instead it was controlling him, and he didn't even know it. Neither did we, at least not to the full extent. It took a host of other things to go wrong in his life for him to come to this conclusion. But he was a prodigal heading in the right direction, even though there were more bumps in the road home and a lot more potholes.

Sometimes Spring Fool Us

Early March
The day spreads out like an empty canvas. What shall I paint? Will I fill it with dark and somber colors or bright red vermillion and cadmium yellows? Shall I define the framework and then paint or should I let Your hand guide me in what to paint? Should I make plans and goals or ride the waves of inspiration? I'm listening to the tinkling wind chimes playing Amazing Grace. They are aptly named.

Dear Lord,
Thank You. You are faithful. Ben's appointment went very well. I spoke to the counselor after, and he believes that Ben has a good chance of overcoming this. He said my son possessed a good faith base, which would help him a lot. The counselor also said that Ben admitted that his drinking in college caused him to fail out. Maybe now he'll be willing to work on that problem since he's admitted to the truth.

Lessons Learned: I didn't realize that in high school and college, Ben had a growing addiction to alcohol. At seventeen he received a DWI, and he went to the required program with his father. I wanted him to see a counselor on a regular basis, but he told me he stopped drinking.

Unfortunately, Benjamin wasn't willing to confront his addiction, even though he initially admitted there was a problem. At least it was a beginning, however feeble it may have been. This was the step he was ready to take at the time. He thought he could do it on his own, though later it proved he couldn't. However, at the time, it gave me hope that he would change, and this was enough to fuel my faith.

March 10th

Faith is a glorious thing. It transforms the landscape of the soul. Two months ago I was in hell, praying Benjamin would walk in God's will, hoping he was alive and not doing drugs. Everyday on the way to work I prayed my heart out, entreating God. As I passed the apple orchard I prayed Ben would bear good fruit. As I passed the bridge, I prayed God would be a bridge of hope for Ben crossing over from a destructive to productive life. As I climbed the hill, I'd prayed my son would draw closer to God. As I waited at the stoplights, I prayed Ben would stop what he was doing and see the light.

Now Benjamin is home, riding in the car with me on his way to his job in the same school I work! I glance over at him, and see God's physical answer to my prayer. He's alive! I'm thankful that he didn't die out there in the streets. I know a Christian woman whose son overdosed on drugs.

Believe me this wasn't what I chose. I wanted Ben to graduate from the college in Florida with a degree in Radiology, but God had different plans. If I focus on his failing out of the school, I'll become sullen and questioning—wondering why Ben had to fall so far down, yet again. It wasn't the first time he failed out of college, but by faith, I believe it will be his last.

Dear Father,

Thank You so much that You brought our prodigal son home alive! He's doing so much better. Thank You that he got that job in my school, and we can ride in together. I pray we will be able to talk about things in his life. I'd like to know why he got into drugs in the first place. Please give me wisdom how to proceed in discussing these things with Ben. Praise God that You answered my prayers, even though it was different than what I wanted. Please help him to have the resolve to stay off drugs. In Jesus' mighty name. Amen.

March 13th

Ben and I have been riding in together almost every day, but he doesn't talk a lot about things. He tells me not to worry—everything will be okay. I've heard that phrase a few too many times. I'm struggling to believe he'll be okay, but it's hard to trust Ben. I know I can trust God, but I'm having difficulty handing over the situation to Him. I worry about Ben. It's my birthday today, and I just want to relax and enjoy life. Why does everything have to be so complicated?

Dear Father,

Help me to see the positive side of this situation. Ben is back, alive and well. Help me to *"Trust in the Lord with all my heart, lean not unto my own understanding. In all my ways acknowledge Him, and He will direct my paths" (Proverbs 3:5).* You know that's one of my favorite verses. I've said it a million times, but now it has new meaning. I'm really being put to the test to trust You with my son. I secretly hoped You would not to require this of me—having severe problems with my children. It's the one thing I feared You would require of me. I can trust You with my own life, but it's completely another issue when I need to trust You with something that is a part of my flesh and blood—my son, yet he is totally beyond my control. Lord, help me to put my prodigal in Your hands and surrender him to You. Forever. Amen.

March 17th

Dear Lord,
I'm so disappointed that Ben's life came to this.
My heart is like a smoldering ember...
Slowly dying out.
It is in need of wood to ignite it.
My heart has grown distant, colder.
My prayers less passionate.
Your wounds, O Lord, have inflicted me.
You have said "No" to my request.

66

You answered them differently;
Much differently than I expected.
Forgive me for my woundedness.
I feel You have transgressed my heart.
Fan the embers of our relationship,
So it may glow again with love.

Lessons Learned: Now that the crisis was over, I had to live with the day-to-day the concerns of life: my husband, my job, my other children and Ben. He was doing well at this point, but his unwillingness to talk about the past was a signal to me that he wouldn't deal with some important issues. Though we couldn't force it on him, I think a little firmer insistence that our son regularly attend counseling sessions and church may have helped to avert or lessen the upcoming blow. Then again, Ben needed to learn his lessons the hard way. Sadly, some people are like that.

Suggestions: Don't get easily discouraged if you or your prodigal doesn't recognize his or her addiction right away or isn't willing to go into a rehab. There are few addicted people who jump at the idea, though some are more willing. Keep praying and suggesting it. Keep probing and asking questions to assess his or her involvement in drugs or alcohol.

Don't let your addicted son or daughter deceive you. If you discover they are using drugs, then put them out of the house if they're not

67

willing to go for treatment or confront the problem. This may take a while depending on the personalities involved and your loved one, but it doesn't benefit anyone in the long run to have a place to stay while they're using. If he or she is willing to get help, then make sure they are accountable to someone on a weekly basis. If necessary, drug test them to prove they're clean, but don't let them know ahead of time. There are products they can use to mask the presence of drugs. Most important—keep them accountable.

March 18th

    Not only have I endured the shame of Ben failing out of school because of drugs, now I have to face the mood swings of my principal. One day she loves the work I do with the children, the next she's angry with me. I wrote this today.

<u>Psalm 23 for Teachers</u>

The Lord is my teacher,
    I shall not lack wisdom.
He makes me to understand His ways,
    And leads me in the path.
He provides rest for my soul,
    And gives me peace…
Even when there is no peace around me.

Though I walk through crowded halls
    And dodge insults,
You will instruct me in the way to go.

I will not fear students or administrators
Your guiding hand will protect me.

You will lead me to a quiet place,
in You,
Cause me to drink deeply.
You will give me peace,
in the noisy classroom,
And in the face of adversaries.
You will calm my troubled soul.

April 15th

It's been almost a month since I wrote. Though it is spring, it is a wintry mix of snow and sleet. Winter is clinging onto us in the Northeast. It's got its stranglehold on us. It's the same with Ben. He keeps clinging to his old ways, returning to his vomit like a dog. He thinks he can shake this on his own, but he can't. Holbrook and I will be talking to a counselor this week about Ben. It's wearing on our marriage.

Dear Lord,

I'm weary of this winter. I want spring to come. Friends tell me Ben's problems might go on for longer, but I don't want to hear that Lord. I want to believe You will deliver him before he falls any further from grace.

Lessons Learned: I wanted Ben to be spared from any more pain and confusion, and get on with his

69

life. But he kept wavering back and forth between his will and God's. Unfortunately, my friends were right to a point. Ben had to fall a little further, to the destruction of his own rebellion and self-will, but not his soul.

Suggestions: Tough love is necessary when dealing with an addict. Don't say something and then do another. Stick to your word and don't give into your prodigal's demands. Try to find out what's really happening and make your decisions based on that. Go to a counselor together with your spouse and decide on a course of action. Plan ahead for several different scenarios so you can be prepared and not get tripped up by your loved one. Addicts are very good manipulators, and they will admit they pull on their parent's heartstrings—so be aware.

April 16th

The freezing rain of April chills the bones and dampens the spirit.

But the presence of the Holy Spirit can drive the coldness out like a warm fire.

The Holy Spirit is a gift of spiritual vitality and warmth in a frozen wasteland.

If the chilling winds never blew, there would be no need for the warmth of the fire, no need to labor for the crackling of wood, no need for heat to chase away the cold.

So too with the Holy Spirit. When the cold winds blow and the icy rains fall, we must kindle the fire of the Comforter.

Come Holy Spirit, set my heart ablaze.

April 18th

Ben is at a prayer meeting and moving in the right direction, though on the weekends he has definitely not kept his promise not to drink. He knows that he can't have a few beers. He's admitted to me that it will eventually lead him back to heavier drinking, yet he goes out and has a few. Maybe he does it to go out and be social with his girlfriend, but I hope he will keep his commitment this weekend.

Dear Father,

Please help Ben to do what he says he will do. Help him not to be wishy washy. "*He is a double minded man, unstable in all his ways*" *(James 1:8).* He thinks he's doing the right thing in his own eyes, but he doesn't know how to judge situations. He is very nonjudgmental and generous to others. I pray You will honor that and balance him out. Teach him to walk in the light of Your ways and not what he thinks is right. "*There is a way that seems right to a man, but its end is the way of death*" *(Proverbs 14:12).* Turn him around. Show him how to be a wise son. Help him to recall what he learned in the past. "*My son, do not forget my law, But let your heart keep my commandment*" *(Proverbs 3:1).* Help me compliment him more. He's writing in a journal and also copying Bible verses. He wants

71

to walk the right path. Dear God, please strengthen him, and show him the way.

<u>Lessons Learned</u>: At the time, I didn't know Ben was addicted to alcohol. My husband and I didn't know his drug problem started with drinking. Once he had a few beers or anything stronger, he lost his resistance to stay away from drugs. He wanted to do what was right, but he just couldn't keep it up for a long period of time. I wasn't sure if he had an addictive personality, and I was trying to see the positive side. However, I desperately wanted him to go for help consistently, but he wouldn't admit he had a serious problem. I was torn in two, trying to figure out what the real problem was, while trying to believe Jesus would take care of it all. Ben was in denial, and to some extent, so was I.

<u>Suggestions</u>: Pursue the truth about your prodigal. When you discover it, don't run away or hide from it. Face it head on with God's help. Try not to fall apart. If your problematic son or daughter is not willing to face the truth, then decide on a course of action and stick to it. Consult others who have experience in the area of your child's difficulty. Plan an intervention with friends or family to convince your prodigal of their need for assistance. Pray and trust God. He is able to bring your wandering child back home and turn this evil around and fashion good from it. Be patient and wait for God to act.

The Ugly Truth

May 30th

Yesterday, Memorial Day, I got smacked with the most crushing news of my entire life. I received a text message from our son's girlfriend. "Ben is a drug addict, and needs rehab." The words stung like a swarm of bees. We were at a friend's graduation party, when I saw this text. My heart sank to the bottom of my soul. It was plain and clear. All my fears had come upon me. Ben was indeed a drug addict!

Dear Jesus,

I don't understand any of this. I hoped and prayed it wouldn't come to this, but You chose not to answer my prayers. Once again, I feel like the psalmist David. *"My God, my God, why have you forsaken Me? Why are you so far from helping mend from the words of my groaning? O my God, I cry in the daytime, but you do not hear; And in the night season, and am not silent" (Psalm 22:1-2).* Lord, I did not keep this pain away from You. I shared it and cried out to You. Please hear me Lord and answer. Help me, Father, to deal with this.

Wake Ben up as you have woken us up to his problem. O Lord, You sent Your son *"to open the eyes that are blind, to free captives from prison and to release from the dungeon those who sit in darkness" (Isaiah 42:7).* I pray You will do so—release Ben from the powers that bind him and form his self-made prison. Release him from the bondages of his addiction and the power he allowed Satan to have in his life through drugs. In Jesus' name. Amen.

June 11th

This was one of the most heart-rendering months of my life. I confirmed Ben's drug problem with his other friends, and they all agree he needs help. He continues to deny that there's a problem. He said he's only smoking pot to keep him off hard drugs. I keep telling him smoking pot is not okay, but he doesn't agree.

Our pastor, Pete, is pushing for us to get him in rehab or tell him to move out. I'm so torn over this. He believes we need to move quickly in getting Ben out of the house. Holbrook has difficulty kicking our son out too. What are we to do?

We took the car away from him, and he didn't come home last night. He's very angry with us, though he's not showing it outwardly. He said he uses drugs because of problems related to his mind and thinking. It drives me crazy. I told him I think it's the drugs that make him think this way.

I see my mistakes so clearly now. I should have listened to my husband more. He didn't want to cosign the loan for the second semester, so Ben wouldn't have been able to go back to Florida. I should have agreed. I feel so guilty. Ben got worse down there. He was lonely and cocaine was too easily available. On top of it all, we'll be responsible for paying off his loan. I was so blind. Now, I see his predisposition towards drugs!

I don't know what to do. I've agonized over this, and realize I need to put Ben in God's hands, Oh, I've done that many times before, but I really, really need to relinquish him. Perhaps, Ben resents me for trying to control him. I'm kicking myself for not letting him take more responsibility earlier in life, though we tried. Now all of us are paying the consequences.

It's time Ben makes his own decisions and pays the consequences for his mistakes. I need to continually place him in God's hands and release both Ben and Holbrook. I can only try to be a good influence. I must find the right balance between a mother's love and tough love.

Dear God,

Help me. I feel as if I'm drowning in guilt, self-pity and confusion. I'm not sure how to think. My mind is filled with conflicting thoughts. I'm trying to trust You. It's obvious we can't trust Ben.

Well at least we know the truth now. We suspected this, but Ben went back and forth so much, we didn't know up from down. You know Lord, we suggested rehab, but Ben thought he could beat this himself. He insisted he wasn't addicted. Yeah, right. I've prayed so hard... but maybe this is an answer to prayer. Maybe it's just better that it's out in the open—Ben has a drug addiction. That cuts like a dagger to the heart.

<u>Lessons Learned</u>: While this was a painful time, God did some needed surgery in my life. I went through a lot of questioning and repenting. The Lord helped me come to grips with some of my attitudes that were wrong. I should have let Holbrook have more control when Ben was younger. It was difficult for me because I didn't trust my husband's judgment on some things. It was challenging trying to determine the right course of action. My husband had a lot of issues and problems of his own. Perhaps I took too much of the upper hand and let Holbrook step out of the picture. All I can do now is repent and try to respect him more.

I felt that if my husband had been more involved with raising the kids, then I wouldn't have stepped up to the plate so much and done what I thought was best. Ben was so sensitive and needed so much love. I thought Holbrook was too hard on him sometimes. Perhaps I should have let my husband discipline Ben more.

I think it would have helped if Holbrook and I had addressed Ben's issues earlier in life—if we had been more aware and known some of the telltale signs: a change of friends, lack of interest in school, irritability, a change of habits and hobbies, and loss of money. However, none of these issues were blatantly obvious when Benjamin was young. There were only subtle changes in him, which took years to become apparent. That's why he was such a tricky case.

When he was in high school, we agreed that Ben needed counseling. He went twice, and the counselor said Ben was okay; he didn't need any more sessions. He sure fooled the counselor and us too. We should have insisted he go back when he started having problems again. I was trying to let Ben make his own decisions, but some of them weren't good ones. Even our younger daughter recognized this.

Suggestions: Facing the truth about an addicted child can bring great turmoil, but remember that God is able to handle this. He can also handle your fears and doubts. Be real with God. He is able to do a great work, if you keep praying and believing. Remember, things are not always as they appear to be on the surface. Look what God accomplished through the death of His Son! He can transform Satan's plans and work miracles.

Dear God,

Please forgive me for being angry with You and saying that You didn't answer my prayers. I know Ben made his own choices. You are not responsible for his addiction. He's stubborn and wants to do things his own way.

77

Help me trust You with him. I'm frightened for him. Maybe he won't ever stop using drugs. Oh, how I wish I saw this coming. Please help me to know how to handle Ben and his addiction. You have always been there for me, helping me through every difficult situation I've faced before.

You are a shelter in the storm, my rock and my deliver. You are *"My refuge and my fortress, my God, in whom I trust. Surely he (You) will save Ben from the fowler's snare and from the deadly pestilence." (Psalm 91:2).* Though Ben has fallen prey to the enemy, I believe You will release him. Lord, I pray for myself now and thank You that *"Surely You will cover me with your feathers, and under your wings I will find refuge; Your faithfulness will be my shield and rampart" (Psalm 91:4).* Lord, still my fearful heart. Help me to keep my eyes on You, to stand firm, trust in You, and release Ben. In Jesus' mighty name. Amen.

July 9th

Today we stood up to Ben and we submitted to what God showed us and what our counselors recommended we do. We said "no" to Ben and the lifestyle he's living. We will not let him continue to live under our roof. This broke my heart.

I remember when he was first born. The pain was tremendous. He was posterior, face up, so he put a lot of pressure on my back. I didn't understand this until later. He seemed like he

78

didn't want to come out into this world, and wouldn't "turn the corner" as the doctor kept saying. I was lying on the table and pushing, but he wouldn't budge. Finally, I gave up and asked the doctor to take me to the operating room to have a cesarean. When I stood up to leave, the baby dropped into correct position, and Benjamin was delivered. I hope and pray that in standing up to Ben, he will wake up and emerge from this darkness.

Dear Lord,

Though I trust You are working in Ben's life, my heart is troubled. Things are not looking good. I fear for Ben. He didn't come home for days, and I'm afraid he's falling deeper into this lifestyle. I can't live like this. He's destroying our peace. He needs to move out. Everyone agrees. Help me to *"Be anxious for nothing, but in everything by prayer and supplication, with thanksgiving, let your requests be known to God and the peace of God, which surpasses all understanding will guard your heart and minds through Christ Jesus" (Philippians 4:6).* Lord, I'm trying to look to You. Please give me peace in all this turmoil. Amen.

United We Stand

July 14th

I don't understand what's wrong with us. We keep waffling back and forth regarding Ben. No sooner did we tell him to leave, then we turn around and help him with the car insurance. I guess Holbrook thought he would need his car to keep his job and be independent. Ben's in a tough place now because of his choices, and we need to stop cushioning the blow, as Holbrook says, but I guess he's as conflicted as me about the best way to handle this situation.

Lessons Learned: Not only did I spend a lot of time in prayer, but I sought counsel from others who were knowledgeable: my sister, those in similar situations, counselors and our pastor. He told me something very important that summer, which stuck with me. If Holbrook and I don't present a united front, and start agreeing on how to handle the situation with Ben, we'll most likely divorce and perhaps lose Ben to this addiction. I'm not sure about the statistics on this, but I know the figures for parents of disabled children. Most of them divorce because of the stress. While Ben wasn't disabled, addiction is considered a disability. God had my attention, and I was open to what He said, even if it hurt. I wanted to try and work things out with my husband. And so I did.

<u>Suggestions</u>: Don't try to figure everything out on your own. Get the help you need. Be flexible and bend to those who know more about these situations. Trust God to show your spouse how to handle things. If you are in disagreement, go to a godly counselor who can guide you. Contact a local rehab (if possible one that is faith based or has a good reputation) and ask to speak with a counselor there. Ask a professional how to handle the situation. And as always, pray!

Dear God,

It's about time we started to do things differently. I believe it's time for me and my husband to combat this evil together. I've prayed these verses many times for all different situations. Now my husband and I need to unite and stand against this evil. "*For though we walk in the flesh, we do not war according to the flesh. For the weapons of our warfare are not carnal but mighty in God for pulling down strongholds, casting down arguments and every high thing that exalts itself against the knowledge of God, bringing every thought into captivity to the obedience of Christ" (2 Corinthians 10: 3-7).* By the blood of Jesus, we come against this power of addiction in Jesus' name, and we cast it away from Ben. We come against any division between Holbrook and me, and we repent of our independence from each other and You. We are completely depending on You, O Lord.

81

Dear Father,

I'm giving You all my fears about Ben. I'm taking all my preconceived notions about how to deal with these circumstances and submitting them to You and my husband. Lord, every time feelings of fear rise up within me, I'm handing them over to You. Guard my heart and my mind. In the name of Jesus Christ and by the power of His blood. Amen.

End of July

Well Ben decided to move in with his girl friend! I can't believe him. He knows that's not God's will for him to live with someone. But it's his own choice. He's going to live with her and her parents. We'll see how that works out. I wonder what kind of parents allow a boy to move in with their daughter? At least I won't have to keep dealing with Ben on a day to day basis. Perhaps it will do him some good to be out on his own, trying to get a job. He says he's going to save his money so they can buy a house. That'll be the day.

Dear Lord,

I don't agree with Ben's decision to live with his girlfriend. He knows how we feel, but I give this situation to You. Perhaps some good can come of it, though I doubt it. "*Your kingdom come, Your will be done On earth as it is in*

82

heaven" (Matthew 6:10). He's in Your hands now. He's out of my control. As for me, *"The Lord is my shepherd. I shall not want. He makes me lie down in green pastures. He leads me beside still waters. He restores my soul" (Psalm 23:1-3).* Thank You Lord that You will provide rest for my soul. In Jesus' name. Amen.

<u>Lessons Learned</u>: God was working in Ben's life through this situation, though I didn't see it at the time. Living with his girlfriend caused Ben to hit bottom and eventually realize he needed help. Though he had to go through a lot more pain and crazy circumstances with her unstable emotions, this finally led Ben back to God.

August

    I went to a dance conference this summer, which opened my eyes to a lot of things—first, the prevalence of drugs among Christian teens and young adults. I met a Christian family from the mid-west at the hotel where we stayed. Their young, innocent looking daughter had just finished a thirty-day rehab for heroin! I prayed with them, and talked a lot with the girl. I could hardly believe such a sweet looking thing was so involved with drugs. During the conference we learned about worship as spiritual warfare and I bought a book, *The Worship Warriors* by Chuck D. Pierce. I'm looking forward to reading it.

    I've also working on my relationship with

Holbrook. I realize part of Ben's difficulty stems from our problems, compounded by his own. Holbrook and I need to work out issues concerning each other and then deal with Ben. It's complicated and sticky, and I need the Lord to help me navigate these turbulent waters.

Dear Father,

I need You now more than ever. I know there are issues in our marriage that need help. Holbrook has difficulty facing some areas he needs healing for regarding his past, and sometimes I don't know how to respond to him. Please help me understand my husband's needs and how to communicate with him. Help Holbrook improve his relationship with his son and me. Please help us to know how to handle Ben and to be unified in our approach. I know we don't always agree. Show us how to compromise a give us wisdom. Help us to *"submit to one another"(Ephesians 5:21)*. Help me give Holbrook the space he needs to work out some of these issues. Show me how to be in an attitude of prayer so that when Holbrook is willing to talk, I will communicate effectively with him. Thank You Lord that *"You will show me the path of life. In Your presence is fullness and joy. In your right hand are pleasures forevermore" (Psalm 116:11)*. Amen.

<u>Lessons Learned</u>: In some ways Ben was totally responsible for his own problems and the choices

he made, yet at the same time my relationship with my husband played into it. Because I didn't understand some communication dynamics, I tried to do good, but actually hurt the situation. I've been reading a great book lately entitled, *Love and Respect* by Dr. Emerson Eggerichs. It has helped me understand that my husband needed more respect than I was giving him.

Perhaps, if I had communicated more respectfully with my husband, then he would have been more involved with raising the children. Whatever the case, I know my marriage needed improvement. I lacked the understanding that a man needs to perceive he's being respected. Even though I thought I was respectful, I didn't always communicate that way. However, I'm happy I now understand that all those times I was trying to help my husband change, he didn't balk just because he was unwilling to change, but rather he was wired that way to perceive it as disrespectful. Now I can truly work on improving my marriage.

September

Friday night Ben called from a courthouse way up North. He was all in an uproar. You wouldn't believe what happened. He wanted me to bail him out from some situation that he didn't explain clearly. I refused, so he went to jail! I wasn't going to get him out of the fix he got himself into, though I was quite distraught at the time. Things are going from bad to worse for that kid—out of the frying pan and into the fire.

He called the next day and explained a little more. He and his girlfriend were arrested on the Canadian border because she was trying to flee the country! I couldn't believe that—flee the country to become a fugitive? What was she thinking? She'd been placed in a psychiatric facility for having fought with a coworker, and she walked out. She then called Ben to come get her and cooked up the idea of fleeing to Canada. He didn't want to do it, but she threatened suicide. Being softhearted (and naïve) Ben followed her plans. Since neither of them had their ID when they tried to cross the border, they were detained. Thank God! Later Ben called from jail and wanted me to come get him, but Holbrook said no. He wanted him to stay there and learn a lesson. This was so hard for me to do, but I agreed.

Labor Day

Dear Father,

I hope I'm doing the right thing, going to see Ben, but you know he's been there for a week. I think he's learned his lesson. Holbrook's really mad at him and wanted him to stay there until his trial, but he reluctantly agreed for me to go up there. Lord, I don't want to do the wrong thing. Show me if You want me to bail him out or just visit him. I come against the powers of

86

darkness that have deceived Ben. In Jesus' name. Help show him that this girl is not a good companion for him. Show him his foolishness. I pray he will listen to us. *"The way of a fool is right in his own eyes, But he who heeds counsel is wise" (Proverbs 12: 15)*. Help Ben to be a wise son and listen to my advice. Amen.

<u>Lesson Learned</u>: Leaving Ben in jail for a week was the best thing to do. Eventually his girlfriend's father bailed him out just as I arrived, but he had a week to think over the situation. He decided to come home with me, though it might have been better for him to go with her family. He told me he would have eventually come home anyway. Since no drugs were involved at the time, we let him back in, which was fine. I thought this would teach him a lesson, and it did—for a little while.

October

I haven't written much since I've been busy with work, and Ben is home safe again. The day I went up to the jail turned out to be almost miraculous. I prayed the whole way. When I got to the jail, I was waiting on line, and they announced Ben's name and a man stepped up to the window. He paid for Ben's release! I wondered who it was, then discovered it was the girl's father! He was there with his wife and was visiting his daughter, Ben's girlfriend. He felt

87

she was responsible for my son being jailed, so he posted bail. It saved me from being the one responsible for getting Ben out. I felt it was an answer to prayer.

On the way home, my son and I talked a lot. We decided to stop by the town where he once attended Christian camp to get something to eat. We sat and looked at the lake and talked. He said he repented—that he would change his ways. Sounded familiar, but I wanted to believe him; just as the father in the Bible believed his prodigal son when he returned home. When the son realized his terrible mistake, he thought:

> I will arise and go to my father, and will say to him, "Father, I have sinned against heaven and before you, and I am no longer worthy to be called your son. Make me like one of your hired servants." And he arose and came to his father. But when he was still a great way off, his father saw him and compassion, and ran and fell on his neck and kissed him. And the son said to him, "Father, I have sinned against heaven and in your sight, and am no longer worthy to be called your son."
>
> But the father said to his servants, "Bring out the best robe and put *it* on him, and put a ring on his hand and sandals on *his* feet. And bring the fatted calf here and kill *it,* and let us eat and be merry; for this my son was dead and is alive again; he was lost and is found." And they began to be merry (Luke 15:18-26).

Like the prodigal son, Ben begged to come home, and promised to do as we asked. We didn't celebrate with a party, but we allowed him back home. After he arrived, we set up a list of rules, such as not staying out at night, not smoking pot, etc. He signed the contract and stuck to it for a few weeks. Now he's started staying out again with his friends. At least he's coming to church, and he seems to be doing better.

Dear Lord,

Please help Ben to keep his promises and to truly repent. He is not well inside, but You are in the healing business. *"Those who are well have no need of a physician, but those who are sick. I did not come to call the righteous, but sinners, to repentance" (Mark 2:16-8)*. I see some changes in him and I'm thankful. I'm trying to put him in Your hands, and believe that *"You will accomplish what concerns him" (Psalm 138:8)*. I'm trying to stand on Your Word, and trust that You will continue to work in Ben's life. You are our helper. In Jesus' name. Amen.

<u>Lessons Learned</u>: As you can see, there were many ups and downs in Ben's life and months when no drugs were involved. However, since Ben never fully addressed his issues, he returned to drugs when things got really bad for him. But I continued to pray and say these verses over and over, believing God would accomplish them and that one day I too could declare like the Father of the prodigal, *"For my son was dead and is alive again."* I waited expectantly for that day, confident that God would accomplish this.

Down a Dark Tunnel

November 3rd

Yesterday I was depressed and discouraged about my marriage and Ben. Holbrook has been snapping at me. Perhaps it's the tension of having Ben back in the house. I found out Ben is smoking pot again. He said he needed to do it once in a while to stay away from hard drugs. When I told him that's not acceptable, he said he wouldn't do it again. I wonder if he's sincere. Is he wrapping us around his finger? He doesn't want to move out, and get caught up with his friend's lifestyle. I don't want him to either, but we need him to obey the rules. He's working and going to school, so he shows some improvement, but he's not doing everything he needs to do to go back to college. It's a constant struggle.

Dear God,

I need Your peace. *"Peace I leave with you, My peace I give to you, not as the world gives, do I give to you" (John 14:27)*. Everything is in constant turmoil. I need to feel Your presence, to know You hear me, to know You love my family and me. Let Your presence be known. I can't live without Your love. I recall the old songs that we use to sing in church. Let me know that their words are true. *"Your love is steadfast and Your mercy never comes to an end" (Lamentations 3:22-23)*. Lord, I cry out for mercy.

90

I need to trust You. Help me to have faith. I'm like the man in the Bible, crying out for more faith. Help Lord, my unbelief! The Psalmist exhorts us to *"Call upon Me in the day of trouble; I will deliver you and you shall glorify Me" (Psalm 50: 15).* I'm trusting You will deliver us and Ben. Send your Holy Spirit to him and refresh me. In Jesus' name. Amen.

November 4th

Dear Father God,

Thank You for answering my prayer. Yesterday, I felt the presence of the Holy Spirit renewing me, showing me Your love. You heard my heart cry and gave me strength to carry on. *"The Lord is my light and salvation, Whom shall I fear? The Lord is the strength of my life; Of whom shall I be afraid?" (Psalm 27:1).* I will not let this fear of my son's drug problems consume me.

I will look at the good things You're doing in my life. Work is going along very well. I really like the building I was transferred too. The principal is very good and the other teachers are very nice. Thank You for their support and encouragement, though they have no idea of what I'm going through. I want to do things Your way Lord, even though the culture shouts out, "Do your own thing."

This is my cross at this time in my life—

my son's addiction. I need to battle with the circumstances and speak faith into it. Help me Father, to have the assurance that you're going to work though my son's addiction. Thank You Lord that your Word assures me, *"You will turn this curse, (my son's addiction) into a blessing (for me and my husband) because You love us"* (Deuteronomy 23:5—parenthetical material mine).

It's strange that for all these years I've been writing a novel about spiritual warfare, and now I have to really live it out and wage war for my son and our marriage.

November 28th

Dear Father,

I know it's important for us to cast our burdens and anxieties upon You Lord, knowing that You care for us (I Peter 5:7), so I cast off Ben's burdens from my shoulders. I cast aside his irresponsibleness, addiction, irrational thinking, independence, rebellion, financial issues, career, problems, inconsistency, personality flaws, and anything else I take on as a burden. I give him to You. I pray Ben will yield to You and *"Will be taught of the Lord and great will be his peace"* (Isaiah 54:3). Thank You for Your peace. In Jesus' name. Amen.

Suggestions: Peace is not an easy thing to attain for most people in this situation. One day you can feel God's peace about the situation and the next be in turmoil. One thing I learned from this is it doesn't matter how you feel! Believe God is at work, even if it's hidden, and you can't see it at the time. Speak words of faith into the situation. Trust God is at work. It will give you more peace, and it can change the outcome.

Early December

Ben didn't come home last night, and I was very worried. He said he stayed at a friend's house because he fell asleep. I don't really believe him. I finally got him to admit he used crack again! What's wrong with him? This seems like a vicious circle. Things go along okay for a while, then he trips again. I need to talk to Holbrook about this. I want to meet with the intake counselor at Transformation Life Center, a Christian drug and alcohol program for men.

Dear God,
Please let Ben see he has a drug problem and needs to go to a rehab. Let him see he can't kick this by himself. Show Holbrook and I how to handle this. Lord, I implore You to show Ben that he needs to go into this program. Reveal to us how to get him to agree.

<u>Lessons Learned</u>:   It was very difficult for both my husband and I to have Ben living at home again. I wanted Ben to follow rules that he was

suppose to follow when he was in his late teens, such as coming home every night. Holbrook didn't think we could require that of him, but I thought if we didn't, he'd go out and drink or do drugs. Ben needed to move out, but we weren't ready to kick him out. To a certain extent, our son wanted to do what was right, but he was going about it the wrong way. We were trying to give him a chance to repent and follow the Lord. Even though he said he repented, he just couldn't walk it out consistently. He'd be okay for a while, then fall down again. But every time he fell, I believe God was bringing him closer to true repentance.

<u>Suggestions</u>: As I said before, try to stick with the plan that you or a counselor come up with, but don't make hasty decisions to please others. If you do change your course of action, try to be in agreement with your spouse. Don't let the addicted person know you are in disagreement. Show a united front. If you are not on the same page, discuss your differences with each other before making a statement to your son or daughter. Try not to let your addicted child put a wedge between you and your spouse. If they do, then work hard to come back together and agree on a plan.

Take advice from others, but know that God works differently in each person's life. Though some people thought that we needed to get Ben out of the house earlier than we did, it worked out that Ben stayed as long as he did. Ben told me later that he would have been far worse off if we hadn't kept trying to help him. He believed we did the best we could, though we could have done some things differently.

December 10th

Holbrook and I met with the intake counselor of Transformation Life Center, and he told us we needed to have Ben call him for an interview. He insisted that if Ben wasn't willing to go there, then we should kick him out of the house—even change the locks if necessary. I asked if we should wait until the holidays are over, and he said no. Holbrook agreed.

The next day we talked to Ben, and he doesn't want to go to the rehab. He said he wouldn't do it again, that he'd get things under control. Holbrook told him he needed to move out, but Ben wanted to stay at least through the holidays. I feel so torn. Should we make Ben leave now?

A few hours later

It seems my husband changed his mind. Oh Lord, this is so difficult. Shouldn't we do what the counselor said, but now Holbrook thinks the man didn't know the whole situation with our son. He believes Ben's not a hard core addict.

At least Holbrook gave Ben a deadline. He needs to move out and find an apartment by

February. I felt better about that anyway, though I'm not really sure it's the right thing to do. Sometimes I'm the one who's too soft, but this time I think it's my husband, but I don't want to let this destroy our marriage. Our pastor warned us that if we didn't work this problem out together, it could ruin our marriage. We've had enough problems already; we really don't need this to add fuel to the fire.

<u>Lessons Learned</u>: As you can see, my husband and I wavered in our plans, yet we didn't allow this conflict to put a permanent wedge between us. God worked things out in the long run, even though we made plenty of mistakes. Give yourself some breathing room. You're not perfect, and you'll make mistakes, but God can take care of even that. Just remain open to what God is doing and don't get angry with each other or with Him. Keep your heart soft and don't let your child's addiction eat away at your relationships. Spend time with each other; enjoy life together, rather than always focusing on the prodigal. Do things that you enjoyed doing before. Have fun, if possible.

A Glimmer of Light

December 17th

God is speaking to me more clearly now that I'm listening. He told me to walk in His mercy and grace. Touch people's lives with grace. Don't be rushed and harried like the world. Move in grace. Overflow in grace towards others. Slow down and stop rushing. These are two things I tend to do, and they cause me anxiety. I believe God wants me to stop focusing so much on my situation with Ben. I need to have peace and share with other about the victories I have.

Jesus doesn't want us to put any relationship above Him and get our peace and joy from them. These words pierce my heart, for this is the work God is doing in my life. I cannot depend on anyone for joy or happiness. I must rely solely on Jesus. He must be my source. It's not that I can't receive joy from others, but Jesus needs to be the root of my joy.

Dear Father,

I praise Your name, O Lord. I lift your name on high. You are the strength of my life. In You I take refuge. I will praise Your name on high for You are worthy to be praised. I will not fear this dark valley You have allowed me to walk through. *"Though an army shall encamp against me, My heart shall not fear" (Psalm 27: 3)*. I trust that You will lead Ben out of this darkness and into Your marvelous light, in Your time frame, not mine. In Jesus' precious name. Amen.

December 22nd

I've been reading Exodus lately, and it's no coincidence. God wants to set us free from our bondages, not only Ben but us too. God wants us to be delivered—me from my worry, Ben from his addictions, and Holbrook from his anxiety and fear.

When Joseph first went to Egypt it started out as a blessing for him and later for his household, then it became bondage for the children of Israel. Our children have been a blessing, but now they are adults. I need to set them free, even if it means they'll make some serious mistakes. Ben should not dominate my life, nor my husband's. We must be set free from him or he will put us in bondage. We must also set Ben free and entrust him to You.

Moses led the children of Israel out of bondage, in spite of his weakness. It took forty years of Moses living in Median before he would begin to fulfill the destiny God had for him. Even then, he believed he was not able to be the mouthpiece of God. He used his brother, Aaron, as a spokesman for him, but even Aaron fell at times. I use to believe God would use Ben. Though sometimes I'm confused as to why all this is happening, I still believe God will use my prodigal son.

The family tree plays a role also in Ben's

98

addiction.

Ben has a weakness due to his heredity. Both our families suffered from depression, and my husband's side with addiction. My side of the family also dealt with personality disorders. Ben fed into the negative aspect of the family tree, but he still had a choice. I believe Satan has used this to get a foothold in his life, but he can still be set free. His battle is in his mind and will. If Ben is to overcome, he must listen to God and obey. He keeps repenting, but then falls again because he's not being completely obedient to God. This is an act of his will. He needs to submit his mind and will to God.

For some this is a great struggle. The flesh wars against the Spirit. In order for anyone to overcome, the Spirit needs to be built up and fed. Reading the Word, believing it, professing it, and praying are keys for being set free. But Ben needs to desire it for himself. I pray that he will wake up and see what he is doing, and desire to do God's will. I believe my son was called of God, and the enemy often tempts those whom God calls. Satan used Ben's weakness to get a foothold in his life.

However, even though Moses sinned and killed a man God used him. He even ran away from God, but later God spoke to him in a burning bush. Eventually, Moses led the Israelites out of bondage.

Dear Lord,

I believe You have called Ben to be Your spokesman, though I don't see this in the present circumstances. However, I am trying to speak the things that are not as if they were, as Your Word encourages us to do (Hebrews 11:1-3). Help me Lord to have the kind of faith that speaks things into existence. My hope is in You Lord, and not in things of the earth. You are my God. You spoke the universe into existence, now I speak my son's freedom from bondage into existence.

You will break the chains of the enemy and set the captives free. As the prophet Isaiah spoke and Your son Jesus said, *"The Spirit of the Lord GOD is upon Me, Because the LORD has anointed Me To preach good tidings to the poor; He has sent Me to heal the brokenhearted, To proclaim liberty to the captives, And the opening of the prison to those who are bound" (Isaiah 61:1-3).* I proclaim that You will open Ben's prison doors. In Jesus' name. Amen.

Lessons Learned: For many years I was involved in spiritual warfare—praying and reading about the spiritual conflict we are engaged in against demonic forces. I even wrote a non-fiction book and a novel on the topic. Though I prayed and battled before, it never hit so close to home as with Ben. In the beginning my prayers were more fearful, but as time progressed I began to trust God more and stand firmer on the promises. Then I began to praise Him, which helped Ben turn a corner.

In addition, a new dimension opened up for me when I began to add dance worship to my prayers. I was involved in Christian dance for years, but not in the sense of personal spiritual warfare. I danced in churches, malls and other public places to proclaim the Lord, and win over the lost, but not for my own family. Going along with some of the principles I learned at the dance conference and in the book *The Worship Warrior* by Chuck D. Pierce. I began to create praise dances to Scriptures and worship songs.

In the beginning, I chose verses from Psalms and created dance moves to praise the Lord. These were usually beautiful and graceful like ballet, but as Ben's problems deepened, so did my dances. I began to trounce and trample the enemy. My dance steps became more warrior like, and I felt the Lord encouraging me to explore further.

Suggestions: The idea of dancing before the Lord and doing battle may be foreign and uncomfortable for you. If it's really not your cup of tea, then it would be beneficial for you to find some praise songs. Listen to them and join in by worshipping God. Let the message of the words sink deep down into your Spirit and get your eyes off your problem and onto God. A great song for this is "Praise You in This Storm" by Casting Crowns (lyrics available on-line).

101

December 30th

I believe God spoke a clear Word to me to continue to come against Satan as Moses came against Pharaoh. Satan does not readily let go of what he perceives to be his. Even though Ben is God's child, as the nation of Israel was the Lord's, Satan is reluctant to let go of what he thinks he possesses. Pharaoh needed to be confronted time and time again, and kept relenting on his promise to let the Israelites go.

I need to continue to pray for Ben that he will see the traps that Satan is laying for him. Drugs are the doorway to witchcraft, and they can allow Satan to get a foothold. Ben needs to see the spiritual battle he's engaged in, but until he does, I need to stand in the gap and pray for him (see Ezekiel 22: 29-31). I need to speak the Word of God over Ben, and believe it will come to pass.

Dear Father,

I thank You that Ben will someday see the light again. I picture him as a child marching up and down the grocery store aisles singing, "I'm in the Lord's army, yes sir. I'm in the Lord's army." I pray that he will once again join your army of prayer warriors and believers. I pray that *"The eyes of those who see (since Ben knew you as a child) will not be blinded and his ears will listen" (Isaiah 32:3—parenthetical material*

102

mine). In Jesus' name. Amen.

<u>Lessons Learned</u>: Reading the Word of God, praying and worshipping formed a tightly woven chord of three strands that were mighty in "pulling down strong holds" (2 Corinthians 10:4). The Word gave me clear examples of spiritual principles to learn from, the promises gave me hope and built my faith, which in turn made my prayers more effective. Praise and worship helped get my eyes off the problem and onto God.

Reading this section over showed me how close to the truth God had brought me. The situation, and all that it entailed, was about to break open. I believe in part, because of the spiritual principles my husband and I put into practice, not to mention the boundless grace and mercy of God.

2008

New Hope

January 2nd

It's a New Year filled with new hope and new promise. Though I need to continue waging spiritual warfare against this evil, I also need to press on and praise God. I've continued to read *Worship Warriors* and it's helped me to see that worship can break the chains of the enemy. The book refers to portals, places where God descends and meets man, such as Jacob's ladder. (Jacob wrestled with an angel whom some scholars believe was Jesus.) I need to stand at the portal and listen to God, to praise and worship Him and to dance. By doing this I allow God to develop His presence in me so that I may walk in God's will and be a vessel for God's presence. I'll be able to put things in perspective, have God's peace and wisdom to know what to do and how to pray.

Dear Heavenly Father,

Thank You for Your Holy Spirit who guides us and for Your Word that holds so many promises. Today I stand on your promise that *"The desire of the righteous will be granted" (Proverbs 10:24)*. I know I'm not righteous in myself, but You have clothed me in Your righteousness because You died for me. I know it is your will that all would come to know and serve you, so I can pray with confidence knowing it is Your will for Ben to repent and serve You. I bind the strongman, his addiction to drugs, so that he will no longer have power in Ben's life. I break this bondage of addiction and drug use. I cover Ben with the blood of Jesus, and pray that he would repent of this sin. In Jesus' name. Amen.

January 20th

Things seem to be about the same. We keep reminding Ben that he's supposed to move out soon. He's spending more time with his friends, whom I don't like, but he says if he moves out than I won't know where he is. I'd rather have him out of the house so I can get some distance from his problems—like his girlfriend.

She calls collect from the jail and talks with him. Ben says he's still in love with her and wants to marry her when she gets out. Doesn't he see she's not the one for him? She's not a believer and suffers from bipolar disorder, plus she's incarcerated! Doesn't he get it? It seems he's doing better as far as the drug problem issues, but I still wish he would go to the Christian rehab center. He went one night and didn't like it. How can he judge by one meeting? He doesn't seem to think rationally at times. We can't force him to go, so he's going to have to move out.

Late January

I joined an on-line ALANON support group. They're helping me understand what I need to do to have my own peace even while Ben is not doing what he should. They talk a lot about the Serenity Prayer. It's somewhat ironic, as I wrote a story about that prayer and it's published. Anyway I pray it almost every day:

God grant me the Serenity to accept the things I cannot change, the Courage to change the things I can, and the Wisdom to know the difference.

I'm trying to be wise—to ascertain the fine line between manipulating and enabling. Both Holbrook and I don't want to enable Ben, but some feel we are doing that by letting him stay. I want him to move out and do as the counselor said, but then I get nervous when Ben says that would be a lot worse, plus I don't want to go against my husband. We can't let this divide us, but it's so very hard.

Feb.13th

Yesterday was a living hell. Looking back over my diary I realized that it was the one year anniversary of discovering Ben dropped out of the Radiology Program.

I was upset because I felt we were being too soft with him. I spoke with his friend, Dan, out of desperation and asked him what I should do. He was concerned also, and said that I should

106

wake him up to what he's doing. I've been trying to do that. But I realize I can't make Ben see. Only God can do that.

I feel guilty that we are not forceful enough, too loving, and that we haven't confronted him enough. Even though we make rules, we just don't stick to what we say we'll do. We gave him a deadline of Feb. 20th. He needs to be out by then. He hardly comes home anymore anyway. He says he's going to move in with his girlfriend. Fine, let him do what he wants. I'm tired of trying to make him do what's right.

Dear Lord,

I give up! I've come to the conclusion that I cannot change Ben. Only You can do that. You're his heavenly father and You know what he needs. He's being rebellious or stubborn, and I don't know what else. You know him better than I do. I release him to You. Take him and all his problems and do what You must. Help me not to fear what will happen to him when I let go. Work repentance into his heart. In Jesus' name. Amen.

Suggestions: Putting your loved one in the hands of God is a difficult thing to do, but it's the best place for them to be. However, it's usually not a one shot deal. You need to do it over and over. It's also not a guarantee that your prodigal will be okay. Your loved one has their own free will to choose his or her path. Yet, when you trust God with the outcome, you will find peace and be able to pray more effectively and not lose heart.

Feb. 23rd

Today I awoke and looked at the sun glittering on the snow like diamonds. I feel it's going to be a new beginning. Hope is stirring in my soul after that week of feeling like I was in hell. I believe God is going to do something good in our family.

Yesterday, Holbrook went to see a counselor with Ben and the girls. This is a positive step for all of them. Ben's drug problem or addiction, I'm never sure quite which it is, has had an impact on them. There are also issues that go way back, but hopefully they will begin to work those out.

Dear God,

I pray that our family can be whole again. I feel like we were so blown apart, not only over Ben, but over issues in our marriage, and in our relationships. I pray for healing of root causes— those things that have influenced my husband to pull away, and caused our son to turn to drugs. Please get down to the deep places in their spirits (Ben and my husband). Touch them with Your mighty hand of love. Bring healing between my husband and the girls. In Jesus' precious name. Amen.

Feb. 25th

Today Ben left to live with his girlfriend's family again. She's out of jail and moving back home. Though I am sad that he is going against God's will, I'm glad that he's leaving. Maybe things can work out with them. The family seems very nice. I've been in communication with them a number of times in the last six months, and they seem like concerned parents and recognize she is mentally unstable. They like Ben a lot and hope things will work out for him and their daughter. The father thinks they're good for each other. I don't. Anyway, there's really nothing I can do to stop my prodigal anyway. He's in God's hands now.

Dear Father,

I pray that You will protect Ben from all evil. Surround him with your angels. *"Let no weapon formed against him prosper"* (Isaiah *54:17).* Let anything that Satan throws in his path, be destroyed. I pray he will eventually come around to seeing things your way. Help him to stay away from bad influences and drugs. I pray this will be a new start for him. In Jesus' name. Amen.

March 1st

During my prayer time today, the Lord showed me that the Word of God reprograms our mind and reorients us to His priorities, like updating a cell phone to a tower. We need to be

109

in the Word to renew our mind, hear clearly from God and get rid of the junk we accumulate in our brain. We need to be built up in faith because the world seeks to tear us down. We need to posses heavenly vision. If we're not looking up at Him, the world will have a field day with us.

Later that week

It's a good thing that the Lord reminded me about looking up to Him. The situation with Ben and his girlfriend isn't good. She left the father's house and now they're living in a hotel until they get an apartment. Ben changed his courses to on-line before he left, but now he doesn't have the availability of a computer as he did at their house. Ben's life keeps going from bad to worse. God is obviously trying to get his attention, but he's not listening.

My Lord,

Open Ben's eyes and help him to see that he is not following in Your will. He once knew you, and he is Your child. Thank You Lord that "the eyes of those who (once) saw will see (again) and the ears that (once) heard will listen" (Paraphrase of Isaiah 32:3—parenthetical material mine). Draw him back to you. Help him to truly repent and to walk in your ways. In Jesus' name. Amen.

April

Ben's situation has worsened. He's working in a factory and had to drop all his courses!

It makes me sick to think that an intelligent child like him, National Honor Society material, can't even get an associates degree. He's doing things his way, and this is the result. The only positive side is that, hopefully, he's staying away from drugs. It appears he is, but how can I really know? Though he often will tell me when I confront him, he's been known to hide things from us also. Well, he's not my problem anymore. I have to detach from him, as the ALANON group recommends. I've hardly written anything in my diary about the whole affair lately. I'm trying to remove myself from my son and let Ben work out things for himself. After all, he's twenty-four years old. I just wish he knew how to handle situations better.

Dear Father,

I need You to help me keep my mind focused on You. I've been speaking with my sister lately and we both agreed Ben has something mentally wrong with him. He keeps shooting himself in the foot. His mind is all confused. Lord, I want to believe. Help me believe *"Your divine power has given us everything pertaining to life and godliness" (2 Peter 1:2)*. You are willing to give him that power. I pray he will receive it. Thank You Lord that you are teaching

111

me to stand firm on Your Word. *"You have given
to us exceedingly great and precious promises,
that though them we may be partakers of the
divine nature, having escaped the corruption
that is in the world" (2 Peter 1:3).* Lord, give me
some assurance that you will indeed turn this all
around. Help me to continue to believe your
promises are true for our lives.

<u>Lessons Learned</u>: Since Ben wasn't living with
us, I was able to see the bigger picture. I was
concerned for his mental stability at this time
because of his continued erratic lifestyle. He just
didn't seem to understand the power of his every
day choices. He wasn't able to see that this girl
was not good for him in the long run. But there
were deeper issue, ones he admitted to me
recently that concerned me even more—like the
deep depression he went through at nineteen,
and his struggle to feel comfortable around
people.

I began to wonder if all his problems
stemmed from heredity, with the depression and
mental instability that ran on both sides of the
family. Yet on the other hand, I saw both Satan
and Ben's own rebellious will at work. These
insights drove me deeper into spiritual warfare
through prayer, dance and worship.

One day in particular, I remember I was
quite discouraged, but God inspired me to dance.
I put my dance clothes on, turned on a Christian
worship CD with several profound worship

songs, and I set my feet and heart to dancing. I trampled on the plans of the enemy and made them mincemeat. Afterwards, I felt like something was going to break—and it did.

It's Always Darkest Before the Dawn

May 17th

It's a good thing I have the Lord and the ALANON on-line group to help me work things through concerning Ben. He's back in town, and both my husband and I don't want him back here—unless he's willing to go to counseling on a regular basis or a rehab. I don't really have a good handle on his drug problem. He seems to be able to stay way from all drugs for months, but then when a crisis hits, he goes back to them.

In my prayer time the Lord spoke to me about a sermon I heard years ago. Dig the trenches and expect the Lord to fill them. I'm not sure of the exact meaning, but I do know it relates to believing God's promises when circumstances look bleak. I need to dig into the promises, dig deep, and really believe them. Then watch God fill them.

I'm going to really need to do this as Ben came home and wants to live here again. He said he'd go to counseling. But can we believe him? He needs to revamp his way of thinking. Who can help him? Does he need the psychologist, the Christian counselor or deliverance? Maybe he needs all three.

Dear Father,

I need to continue to believe You will heal Ben. His way of thinking is all screwed up. He thinks the strangest things about himself. Only

114

You can heal him. Please dig up the hard places in his life and fill them with your blessings. Heal his mind, his spirit and his soul. *"The Lord is close to the brokenhearted and saves those who are crushed in spirit"* (Psalm 34:17). I am brokenhearted Lord, but Ben is crushed in Spirit. Save him from himself.

Help me to surrender all my fears...those are my rocks, my burdens. I need to replace them with faith. Help me do this dear Lord. In your precious Son's name. Amen.

Suggestions: Surrendering is a process. Don't feel guilty if you give the problem over to the Lord one day and take it back the next. Repent and move forward. Don't let guilt stop you in your tracks. Jesus is always ready to hear our confession and forgive. Sometimes, it's two steps forward and one backwards. Just keep moving on in faith.

June

Its obvious Ben is engaged in a great battle, not only against evil, but the sin that is within, and the flesh that wars against the spirit. *"For the flesh lusts against the Spirit, and the Spirit against the flesh; and these are contrary to one another, so that you do not do the things that you wish"* (Galatians 5:17). There is a side of Ben that wants to do good, but there's a side that keeps choosing to do wrong.

115

Our pastor, Pete, counseled us to cut Ben off. Tell him we love him, but let him know we will not tolerate anymore of his empty promises. I believe God will bring Ben though this. A light at the end of the tunnel exists, but how long Ben stays in the dark depends on him, and his willingness to surrender to God.

The best alternative for him would be to go into the Christian drug program at Transformation Life Center, before he gets totally addicted, hard core, and before he wastes anymore time. I've heard it's a great, Bible based program with a high success rate.

The only other alternative I know of in the areas is an outpatient program, First Step. He would need to go at least three days a week, which he'd likely skip out on. So he'll probably need to find another place to live.

Dear Lord,

My husband agreed. Ben needs to find another place to live if he won't go into a rehab program. Help us to stand firm in this. Lord, help me to *"Be anxious for nothing, but in everything by prayer and supplication, with thanksgiving, let your requests be known to God and the peace of God, which surpasses all understanding will guard your heart and minds through Christ Jesus" (Philippians 4:6).* Lord, give us Your peace that surpasses our own understanding, knowing that Ben may need to fall even further into darkness. If this be the case, I believe You will pluck him out of the darkest hole he has dug for himself. You are able to do great and mighty things. In Jesus' Mighty name. Amen.

Life Sustaining Scriptures and Promises:

I continued to claim these following verses daily. I personalized them and thanked God that He already accomplished this.

• *"You will turn this curse (of addiction and drugs) into a blessing for us because you love us" (Deuteronomy 23:5—added material mine)*. I believed that part of Ben's problem was an addictive personality that in some ways is a curse of inheritance, but I also wondered if my husband's family had a curse on them, as we had seen this early in our marriage during times of prayer. In addition, I believed Ben brought a curse upon himself by being involved in drugs, but I prayed against this and bound it. I used this next scripture as a reference and promise, *"whatever you bind on earth, will be bound in heaven" (Matthew 18:18)*.

• *"You look upon his (Ben's) affliction and trouble and forgive all his sins" (Psalm 25:18—parenthetical material mine)*. Ben was afflicted. He spoke of this often. He felt he was obsessive compulsive and that something was wrong with his brain.

117

Trouble followed him no matter where he went since he started getting into alcohol and drugs.

- *"Lord, You will acquit him (Ben) of hidden faults" (Luke 6:18—parenthetical material mine).* He has secret areas of his life, he is holding unto. Places he is hardly willing to open up about. I believe that you will open up these areas of hurt and heal him.

- *"May you (Ben) be filled with the knowledge of His will in all wisdom and spiritual understanding, that you (Ben) will walk worthy of the Lord, fully pleasing Him, being fruitful in Him" (1 Colossians 1:9 and 10—parenthetical material mine).* I prayed Ben would be fruitful and used of the Lord.

<u>Lessons Learned</u>: Finding scriptures and promises that related to Ben's situation helped me through my darkest hours. Meditating on them had the added benefit of growing my faith and comforting my spirit. Repeating them over and over helped me to keep my prodigal in God's hands on a daily basis. Trusting their author changed my heart.

"For the word of God is alive and powerful. It is sharper than the sharpest two-edged sword,

cutting between soul and spirit, between joint and marrow. It exposes our innermost thoughts and desires" *(Hebrews 4:12 NLT).*

Not only did God fulfill every promise above and beyond what I could imagine, but He changed my heart in the process. I believe beyond a shadow of a doubt that God will fulfill His Word. It may not be in our timing or in the way we expected, but God's Word does not come up empty.

Light at the End of the Tunnel

June 19th

Alleluia! Alleluia! Praise the Lord!! Ben finally agreed to go to the outpatient program at TLC. This is such an answer to prayer. I drove him there yesterday for an interview. Though they wanted him to go as an inpatient, they're allowing him to be an outpatient. Thank You Lord.

It took a lot for him to take this step. He needed to come to the end of his rope. His girlfriend turned on him, and he went back to using crack. Then his license was taken away because he was driving without insurance for several months. I tried to warn him, but he wouldn't listen. But it doesn't matter now. He's willing to go into the program. I only hope he will stick to it.

Dear Father,

Thank You for helping Ben make the right decision. "*Great is your faithfulness O Lord. Your mercy, O LORD, is in the heavens; Your faithfulness reaches to the clouds*" *(Psalm 36:5)*. Thank you that he is taking a step in the right direction. I pray he will follow through and keep his word. I hope he will allow Your Word to heal him, soften his heart and correct his twisted way of thinking. Please let this be the start of a brand new day for my son!

120

June 22nd

  After reading so many Psalms that comforted me, I decided to write my own. Actually, I was inspired by the Holy Spirit to write this.

A Psalm for My Son, Benjamin

O God, my God,
Hear my cry.
The cry of a mother,
  Weeping for her son.

O Lord, my Lord
Only You can break the bondages
of the evil one.
Only You can soften Ben's hard heart.

Send the rains of your mercy
  And goodness,
   to soften his parched soul.
Send the fire of the Holy Spirit
  to burn away deception.

Let him bow his knee before You.
Let tears stream from his eyes
  Repentance from his heart.

Break the teeth of the snake
  who bit him.
Crush his head,
  With Your scepter.

Detoxify Satan's ugly poison
in my son's body.

Break the chains of
        Addiction encircling him,
        the chords which have bound
            his hands and feet.
    So they may no longer run to evil.

Let His heart burn with the
        Fire of Your holiness.

Embrace him with Your love.
Bind the chords of Your commands
        Around his heart.
Let Your Word be ever before him.
            Renew his mind with Your Word.
Heal his thoughts and his spirit.

Destroy the webs of deceit that have
        confused his thinking.
Obliterate the carefully laid plans of
        Satan and his minions.
Take back what is rightfully Yours!

He is the son of Your right hand,
        Benjamin.

    His inheritance is in You—
    Restore his portion and renew him.
Fill his cup that it may run over.
    Anoint his head with the oil of

Your Holy Spirit.

Teach him Your ways, O Lord.
Direct his paths to You.
Use him for Your plans and purposes.
Smash the head of the enemy.
Restore unto him the joy of
Your salvation and
Renew a right spirit within him.

May Ben go out and take back
what is rightfully Yours.
His inheritance in You.
May he go into the Promised Land
and dwell there.
Forever and ever. Amen.

<u>Big Lessons Learned</u>: A year and a half after I'd written this, I see how much God brought all of this to pass. I'd forgotten this personalized Psalm as it was tucked away in my journal, but I found it today. It's amazing how God answered every single cry of my heart, and this poem sums it up. Benjamin is now on fire for the Lord, and talks about his freedom in Christ wherever he goes. All the confusion and heartache in his life is gone, like a vapor. The poison of the drugs left his body and mind. He thinks clearly and is enrolled in a challenging program at school. God smashed the head of the enemy—completely.

God hears the cry of our heart. When we

pray according to His Word, He will indeed answer. Putting all our concerns in God's hands is the best way to trust God and achieve peace in difficult circumstances.

June 30th

Praise God! Ben completed a full week at TLC (Transformation Life Center), and he likes it. He's going faithfully every day. I pray he keeps it up.

I think the greatest lesson I learned is to surrender everything to the Lord. Ben is in God's hands and so are my other problems. I could worry over Ben not wanting to complete his six months commitment, but I'm not going there.

I use to fear for Ben knowing how sensitive he was, and how this could develop into a life-long problem. But God helped me to face this fear. It caused me to spend many hours in prayer. Though we are not out of the woods yet, I'm going to *"Walk by faith and not by sight"* (2 Corinthians 5:7).

I read an entry in my journal for July in which the Lord called me to be like porcelain. Porcelain clay is finer and more transparent. It goes though the hottest firing temperatures of over 2,300 degrees. The clay and the glaze become one to give the translucent effect. My prodigal son's drug problems put me in the hottest furnace I've experienced, and God in his faithfulness brought me through it. I pray that I can radiate the love and compassion of God to those who are hurting or in similar circumstances. I want to be translucent china and reflect the image of God to a hurting world.

Dear Father,

Thank You that Ben is attending the TLC program and it appears to be having a positive effect. *"For You, Lord, are good, and ready to forgive, And abundant in mercy to all those who call upon You" (Psalm 36:5).* Thank You Lord that he has surrendered to You. Help me trust that You will heal him of his addictions. Thank You, for I can now see the light at the end of this dark tunnel. Thank You that You shined Your light on Ben and he saw it. *"The people who walked in darkness have seen a great light; Those who dwelt in the land of the shadow of death, Upon them a light has shined" (Isaiah 9:2).*

You are the light, Lord Jesus. In you there is no darkness. Lead Ben into the fullness of your light and show him how to leave the darkness behind him. Show us, my husband included, how to proceed from here. Help us to take one step at a time, one day at a time. In your precious Son's name. Amen.

End of June

Dear Father,

It's been so nice when Ben comes home

from TLC. I ask him about what transpired, and he shares what he's learning. Everything in the program is based on the Bible. Even though he's only there for two hours a day, it's already having an impact on him. I'm so thankful that he gets up every day and goes. Thank You for answering my prayers. I pray Ben will *"Not conform any longer to the pattern of this world, but be transformed by the renewing of your (his) mind. Then you will be able to test and approve what God's will is—his good, pleasing and perfect will"* *(Romans 12:1—parenthetical material mine)*. Show him how to think clearly and to see things as they truly are. Please set his mind straight. Help him to see truth. I thank You God that *"You did not give him a spirit of fear, but of power and love, and a sound mind"* *(2 Timothy 1:7)*.

July 2nd

Ben was doing so well, and yesterday was a setback of sorts, but thank goodness he didn't do any drugs. His girlfriend came up, and messed up the evening. He took her to the fireworks, and she left him because she got mad at him for something stupid. Then when they both got back here, she wanted to leave. He begged her to stay, but I wanted her to go. It was so sad to watch him crying that she was breaking his heart. He really loved her, and she treated him so poorly.

Dear Lord,

We've tried to be kind to Ben's girlfriend, but she has major emotional problems. I pray he will see she's not the right one for him. I know it's hard because he told me they planned on getting married on her birthday in July, but I don't think it would have worked out. She's not a committed Christian, though this Easter she supposedly accepted Jesus into her life. I've tried talking to her about You, but she has little understanding. She is a troubled young lady, and I pray she'll get the help she needs. Please heal Ben's broken heart. I hope this shows him that she is not the one for him. Though he has problems of his own, he is a very kind and gentle soul. Help him to get things right in his relationship with You. In Jesus' name. Amen.

July 5th

My husband and I went to a picnic with Ben that TLC hosted. It was very nice, until the end. Ben got really annoyed about this kid who was bothering him at the program—doing things like throwing spitballs and being disrespectful. Ben said the guy talks when the speakers are teaching. My son got annoyed with the director and kind of told him off. Ben said they should run the place more strictly and not allow guys like that kid in there.

I spoke with Ben about this young man before and explained that it's not only a program for Christians. He needs to remember this guy was a former drug addict. I asked Ben to pray for him and the situation. My son was annoyed, but he said he would.

Dear Lord,

I can't believe it! Ben came home and told me he apologized to the guy about getting so angry at him! What a change in Ben's attitude towards this guy. He didn't know what to do and was so surprised by Ben's actions. My son said he's been much nicer to him and more respectful in general. Thank You Lord for working so quickly in Ben's life. He was so willing to back down. I see such good changes in him. Thank You for breaking through to him. Amen.

Lessons Learned: God was working quickly in Ben's life because he was now willing to submit to Him. The things he learned as a child were hidden in his heart, and being at TLC was bringing them back to life. The principle of proverbs was showing itself to be true. *"Train up a child in the way he should go, and when his is old he will not depart from it" (Proverbs 22:6).* The Proverbs are not promises, but general principles—observations about life. Although Ben departed for a while from truth, like the prodigal son, he came back! God is merciful.

July 8th

I wrote this poem in response to what God did in Ben's life.

Rejoice

I will make a joyful noise
and shout:
Praise to the Lord!
For His Mighty Hand
is able to save.

He has plucked my son
from the nets of the enemy.
He has broken the neck of addiction.
His Word is truth.
It does not come back void.

You have brought my son
back from the dead.
Stand him upright,
So he may walk
steady in your ways.

Teach him to stay
on the path of life.
Cause his feet to run away
from evil desires,
and pursue righteousness.

Let nothing stand between
You and him.
Let not his enemies regain entrance.
Though they lurk
in the background.
Utterly destroy them!

129

Put a guard over
>   Ben's mind and heart.
Let him desire goodness and the
>   Fruits of Your table.
Let him eat and be full from
>   The truth of Your Word.

Bring healing to his broken spirit.
Bind up the chords of his heart.
>   Anoint his head with oil.
Fill him with your Holy Spirit
>   that he may speak your truth.

Destroy all the works of darkness,
>   that he may proclaim—
>   The goodness of the Lord.

<u>Lessons Learned</u>: God worked miraculously in Ben's life, and I wanted to praise Him for it. I believe that thankfulness is very important. We should be thankful for all the blessings we enjoy here in America, and especially when we see God's miraculous hand at work. Most of all, we should simply be thankful for who God is and what He has done for us though His Son.

<u>Suggestions</u>: Though your prodigal may go through many ups and downs, maintaining a thankful heart for the glimmers of hope is not being naive. It is learning to trust God in the good times and the bad. I recommend you do this everyday, no matter what is happening.

Praise

Mid July

Ben got a job with his good friend who lives up the road. Since my son lost his license, they drive in together. It's working out well. Ben goes to TLC in the morning, comes home and then talks with me. We discuss all kinds of great things God is showing him. Ben has a deep understanding of God and insight into His ways. However, I don't like that he goes out once in a while to the bars, but he seems to be keeping things under control. He won't have more than one or two beers because he realizes any more than that gets him in trouble. I wish he'd avoid it altogether, but where else is there for a twenty‑five year old boy to meet with friends besides church? He attends services every week and reads his Bible every day, and I'm thankful for that.

Dear Father,

Thank You so much for the work You are doing in Ben's life. I can see he's thinking more clearly and understanding a lot about you. Continue to lead him and guide him in the way he should go. Open his eyes to your ways. Please continue to give him understanding in leading a godly life and in staying away from drugs. Help him to be a wise son, as the proverbs encourage young men. *"Wisdom is the principle thing,*

131

Therefore get wisdom" (Proverbs 4:7), and *"My son, keep your father's command, And do not forsake the law of your mother"* (Proverbs 6:20). Thank You for the TLC program and what You are doing in Ben's life. In Jesus' Name. Amen.

End of July

Ben completed six weeks in the program, and is doing very well. He recently opened up about a lot of things. My prodigal has finally realized he's the kind of person that has to completely stay away from drinking, even one beer. He said that if he has one then in a couple of weeks he'll have more, then he'll start on the downward spiral—that's what being an alcoholic is all about, that's where Ben's addiction starts. I thought he only had a drug problem, but he mainly did them once his defenses were lowered through alcohol. It all makes sense now. I hope he can keep this under control, or more correctly I should say, I hope he learns how to give this to the Lord on a daily basis. He also realizes that Alicia is not the right girl for him, though he says he still loves her. He's beginning to see things more clearly.

Lessons Learned: Much of Ben's confusion and risk taking behavior stemmed from the drugs and alcohol. This was not who he was by nature. He was a little shy, and this prompted him to

132

drink to make friends. Drinking lowered his defenses and then he would allow himself to take drugs. This was where it all began—alcohol.

At first we were unaware of our son's drinking. Though I questioned Ben about his whereabouts, he was very good at covering things up. When we discovered he was drinking and smoking pot, he said he would stop, and he did for a while.

We should have dug deeper and confronted Ben more about his problems, where he went and what he did as a young teenager— when we had more control in his life. Though we tried, he was evasive. I advise you not to let your son or daughter evade you. Probe. Follow up on what they say. Once our son went away to college, we had less influence over him and drinking took over more than we knew.

Suggestions: Parents need to be careful if their teen has a shy personality and drinks to fit in with the crowd. Or perhaps they are very social and go out drinking with their friends. Don't think this is just normal teen behavior. Nip it in the bud before it develops into a full-blown addiction. Find social outlets and develop their talents. Sports, music and the arts as well as after school clubs are all good avenues for them to channel their energy and find friends. At the same time, be careful of your son's or daughter's associates. Remember the old adage—one rotten apple spoils the whole bunch. In other words, bad company corrupts good morals.

At the same time it's not healthy to smother or stifle your teenager too much. Give them freedom a little bit at a time so they can test the waters. Have them invite friends over so you can see who they choose and later discuss their choices. As they make wise decisions, give them more freedom and responsibility. Pull back when they make poor choices.

Dear Father,

Thank You that Ben has begun to see the light. He's got a long way to go, but I'm grateful he's on the right path. I believe the Holy Spirit will teach Ben everything he needs to know pertaining to life and godliness (2 Peter 1:3 paraphrased). Thank You Lord that You have opened his eyes to the truth. *"Sanctify them (our Son) by your Word. Your word is truth"* (John 17:17—parenthetical material mine). Give him a continual hunger for more of You. Not just for a season, but for the rest of his life. In Jesus' name. Amen.

August

Everyday I see more and more of my prayers answered. Ben is doing so well. He's been very disciplined, something he lacked as he got older. He continues to go to the program everyday and share with me. He's helping out around the house more than ever before.

Ben is doing a great job of painting the window trim and completing whatever I ask of him. He's also working and is a very good employee. Everyone really likes him. Ben has always been well liked by the people he works with because he is so kind. But now, he's sharing his faith and being a good employee. He sings for them at their request, and he's been really enjoying it. It's wonderful to see him happy and not so self-conscious and apathetic about life. I love seeing him coming back around.

Dear Jesus,

Praise Your name, O Lord, for Your name is high above the heavens. You are worthy to be praised. Your praise will continually be on my lips. As in the story of the prodigal son, You rescued Ben from the path of destruction, and I will praise Your name forever and ever. I stand in awe of You; how quickly You have moved, after these years of sorrow and devastation. I praise You and pray that You will *"Restore the years that the locust has eaten" (Joel 2:25).*

September

I'm back to work, and don't have as much time for Ben. I'm so thankful I had part of the summer with him, and I was able to be around when he came home from the program. His three month suspension of his license will be over soon.

He wants to buy his friend's mother's car. She said she'd sell it at an incredibly low price of $500. He's been paying his bills with his small salary and doesn't have any money. I told him last month if he wanted to buy it, he'd have to earn it by working on the house. Well he finished painting, stacking wood, cutting the lawn ad doing everything else we asked of him. Holbrook and I are pleased with how he is doing, as well as the program director, but they still want him to go in full time. He hasn't mentioned anything about this, and he plans on working full time this winter, saving money for college, and going back to school. I think that's a good idea.

Dear Father,
Thank You for all the work You're doing in Ben's life and in ours. Day by day, I see You answering my prayers. Ben is doing well, better than in years. Though he needs to deal with some of his issues, he is opening up a little more. Thank You Lord that You will complete the good work You began in him (Philippians 1:6 paraphrased). Help me be patient. Give me wisdom how I should approach him.

End of September

Ben completed all the work we asked him to, so we gave him the $500 for the car. He saved enough money to register and insure it. Now he can work some overtime, and get to TLC more easily without depending on my husband and I. The Lord worked out all the details for him as he submitted more to our authority, the leaders in the program and at church. God is blessing him. I'm learning to pull away and place Ben more and more in God's hands—something that was very difficult to do when he was having so many problems. Now I see that I was trying to control my son to a certain degree. I didn't want him to have to fall so far, but he had to do what he had to do.

Ben believes God *"Works all things together for good for those who love him, and are called according to his purposes" (Romans 8:28).* I believe that too, but sometimes I wish Ben hadn't gone through so much.

<u>Lessons Learned</u>: Though there are things we could have done differently—the would have's and should have's that I've written about, I do believe God worked everything out for good. He took all our mistakes and wove them into the fabric of Ben's life to eventually create a beautiful tapestry. As stated before, don't come under condemnation for what you may have done wrong. God can fix it, but be willing to learn and try things His way.

<u>Suggestions</u>: It's difficult for a parent to watch their child make so many mistakes and fall so hard. We want to shelter them and step in, which is okay when they're young, but not when they

get older. It takes wisdom to know when to let your child fall and make his or her own poor decisions. If we allow them to do this more while they're still living at home, it might teach them some important lessons. Real life consequences at a young age can be a very good teacher.

Dear Lord,

Thank You that You *"Uphold all who fall. And raise up all who are bowed down" (Psalm 145:14)*. You have lifted Ben up by your mercy and grace. You didn't allow him to stay in the hole and die there. You picked him up. *"And lifts the needy out of the ash heap" (Psalm 113:7)*. Thank You so much for your mercy. *"Oh, give thanks to the Lord for He is good! For His mercy endures forever" (1Chronicles 16:34)*. Thank You Lord that You had mercy on me and my son. I will be eternally grateful. In Jesus' name. Amen.

Restoration

October

Ben told us he would like to go into the program full time! Initially, I was confused and a little annoyed. He just got the car, is doing well at work, and planned to go back to school in January. At first, I didn't get why he wanted to do this. He changed his mind so quickly. Ben said one of the reasons was that the other guys were jealous since he has the freedom to leave every day. He's the only one in the outpatient program. But I don't think that's a good enough reason. I called the program director and he thinks it's a great idea. He said Ben would get a lot more out of the program by living there and interacting more with the guys.

Holbrook thinks it's a good idea too, so I'm going to go along with it. We'll have to pay all his bills—college loans, credit cards, and car insurance. It seems like a lot of money on top of paying for the program, but it's what we wanted in the beginning for Ben.

Plus—I'm trying to let Holbrook lead in this and agree with him. It's not an easy thing for me to do. Holbrook thinks it will be good for Ben to get more grounded in the Word and in the principles they are teaching at TLC. I guess he's right. I need to trust Holbrook more and not take all of this on my shoulders. After all, I was the one who pushed for Ben to go back to school

139

against my husband's better judgment and look where that got us—NOWHERE fast.

Dear Lord,
You know this is difficult for me—to do something I don't totally agree with, but I'm trying to submit to Holbrook. I pray You will lead Ben in this. You know I want him to continue his schooling, and he finally wants to, now this. I hope this doesn't knock him off track. But then again—maybe You have something different in mind that I don't see. Help me to trust You Lord and increase my faith. In Jesus' name, Amen.

Lessons Learned: I thought I knew what was best in raising our children (two daughters and a son), but boys are different than girls and sometimes need a firmer approach. I should have let my husband lead more in this area and not have been so soft on the consequences. It takes real wisdom, insight and humility to know what is best for each of your children. Listen to those who God puts in your life, if they are following godly principles.

November

I went to one of the graduation ceremonies at TLC (Transformation Life Center) last night. It was very powerful. God completely turned around the young man who was graduating. I heard his testimony the week before. When he first came up to the podium to speak, I thought, *Oh boy here comes a real burnout.* Then he began to tell his story. He was articulate and intelligent. Boy was I convicted. It turned out that he use to be a teacher (like me), and so now I have a special affinity with him.

I also met a young man, Mark, who I sat next to because there were no seats near my son. I introduced myself and we were engaged in conversation. He seemed lost. When I asked him if he ever went to church, he broke down crying and told me he use to go then he fell way. He continued to cry and then turned around and hugged me.

Since then I've seen him a few more times, and we've spoken a lot. He has a sweet and gentle spirit. He is growing closer to the Lord, reading his Bible. He looks so much happier and at peace. God is restoring him.

Thanksgiving

We have so much to be thankful for, especially for the work God is doing in Ben's life. Today we went to a retreat center, associated with TLC, to have Thanksgiving with Ben and some of the other members and their families. I got to meet Mark's mother. He seemed so happy to have her and his father there. He informed me that they haven't talked to each other in years. I told him I would pray for them.

141

Ben is doing so well. We had a nice Thanksgiving dinner and then went for a walk. At first, the girls didn't want to have dinner up there, but it worked out well. It's so beautiful up there, on top of a mountain. We enjoyed a brisk walk together. My heart was at peace.

December

Well it's been a blessing for Ben to be in the program full-time. Holbrook and I are now going to services there on Sunday. He really likes them. The worship is good and the speakers are dynamic. Ben is learning a lot from these people, and I am learning to love these boys.

My heart reaches out to them. Each Sunday one of them shares their testimony. They are both powerful and heart wrenching. What some of these boys and men have gone though, makes you want to cry. Some had very difficult lives, and others grew up in Christian homes and turned away from God, deceived by Satan. Yet, their stories of God's redemption and transforming power are so wonderful. Truly this is a Transformation Life Center!

Dear God,

I feel so richly blessed these days. You have given us so much, and I want to give back to You. Thank You Heavenly Father that all things are in your hands and in You *"All things hold together" (Colossians 1:17 NIV)*. Your ways are high above my ways. This was your plan, not mine, to bring healing and wholeness to Ben. Thank You that You will (continue to) show (Ben) the path of life (paraphrase of Psalm 116:11).

Lessons Learned: God is indeed using this whole terrible ordeal with Ben to work things out for His purposes. My son could have chosen an easier path, but God is taking this whole mess and transforming it into something good. Though there are things we could have done differently, it's difficult to say whether or not we could have prevented this.

Ben believes this was the path he needed to go down. He said he had to learn the hard way. Some of us do. So even though I can give you some suggestions and advice, it doesn't mean that it will prevent your loved one from choosing a wrong path. There are no guarantees. However, the Word of God is true, and you can stand on it. But everyone's story is different. God is not into formulas, but principles. He works with all of us individually.

Christmas

Ben came home for a couple of days. It was good to have him around again. We spent Christmas Eve together with Holbrook's sister, and then they came to a Christmas Eve service with us for the first time. The boys and men from

143

TLC planned on going to this meeting, but it was purely coincidental. We attended the service because my husband, my daughter and I were in a taped choreography of the song "America", (While You Were Sleeping) by Casting Crowns. I was glad my sister and brother-in-law agreed to come. We don't often discuss spiritual issues anymore. We just try to live out our Christianity, rather than talk about it. So it was good for them to come.

Some of the guys from TLC came over to say hello to Ben, and I introduced them. I'm praying that the whole evening will have a positive impact on Holbrook's sister.

On Christmas we went to my sister's house. Some of the relatives know that Ben is in a program. This is one of those Catch 22 situations. Here we are the born-again members of the family, and our son is the only one who winds up in a drug rehab. My sister's relatives were terrors when they were younger, and they all straightened out and became cops. My son, the Christian, becomes the drug addict. My nephew, who had some difficulty in high school, is going on to law school, while my son, the bright one of my family, hardly has his associate's degree. It just makes me shake my head and wonder at the unfairness of it all, but I know that's looking at things from a human perspective. I need to keep my eyes on the Lord and have His point of view.

144

Dear God,

I'm not feeling so full of faith right now. I'm sorry. I feel a little envious. I know jealousy robs my joy and dampens my relationship with You. It's just that the situation hurts. I raised Ben as a Christian, and he gets involved in drugs. I just wonder sometimes what kind of testimony this is to my family. When I was raising young Benjamin, my sister thought I quoted the Bible too much in disciplining him. She hardly brought her kids to church, and they turned out great. I feel like a failure. I know those are feelings I dealt with before, but they're still lurking under the surface. I need Your strength right now. Help me Lord not to drown in them. Amen.

December 27th

I'm feeling much better today. Though I love Christmas, it brings a lot of stress with it. Holbrook is feeling much better too. He doesn't like Christmas at all. He has a lot of bad memories from his childhood. I hope some day he deals with it. This year he went to a counselor, so he's making progress.

Ben came with us today up to Mohonk Mountain House. It's such a beautiful eclectic, Old World resort. I love all the rooms decorated for Christmas in Victorian style. We took a lot of pictures. It was nice to have our whole family together. I love being with my family and seeing everyone happy together. The girls and I went skating together, which is good for us to have special times with each other. I'm looking forward to going to New York City with them and a good friend. Ben has to get back to TLC today, so he won't be coming.

Dear Father,

Thank You that *"In your presence is fullness of joy. At your right hand are pleasures forevermore" (Psalm 16: 11).* I lost sight of this a little, but You made it clear again. It was so nice to see my old friend from high school and have fun together with her and my daughters. She's been through a lot also, and she loves you too. We talk a lot and lean on each other. It's so important to build each other up in the faith. I'm so glad for the support in your family. Thank You Lord that our riches are not here on earth, but in heaven. Help me to keep sight of that. In Jesus' name. Amen.

Lessons Learned: It's yet another year later, and I'm finishing writing and editing this book. I marvel at how God works. All the questions and frustrations I felt last year are gone because of the way the Lord worked everything out. I no longer feel that Ben is a poor witness. He is a testimony of God's power to change people's lives and transform situations.

Because of Ben's addiction, I've been able to minster to many people and my own extended family. I wrote a book of testimonies from twenty-seven of the men who went through the program at TLC, entitled *Transformed, Inspiring Stories of Freedom.* (By the way, you can check out TLC's web-site at tlc911.org.)

Ben's addiction also opened the door to ministering to other families with similar problems and to others on-line. God certainly used my son's experience for good, not only in his life, but in mine.

Like the parent of the prodigal son, I am rejoicing in the return of the wayward son God returned to my husband and me. He is now all, even more than what I envisioned he would become.

2009

True Peace

January 1st

I had a wonderful New Year's Eve alone with the Lord. I lit the candles around the house, turned on some Christian music and felt God there with me. It is His presence that has gotten me though this entire ordeal. I feel such peace in His company, even with the many unanswered questions about Ben's life for the future. I am learning how to place them in God's hands.

Dear Lord,

Thank You that You give us the *"Peace that surpasses understanding" (Philippians 4:7).* According to my sisters, I should be cautious about believing that Ben won't struggle with this issue of drugs for the rest of his life. Sure, this is a fear, but I'm placing this fear in your hands. I believe your Word over the wisdom of this world. Like the psalmist David, *"I called upon the Lord in my distress and cried out to my God: He heard me from his Holy temple...He delivered me from my strong enemy,* (the power of drugs in Ben's life) *the Lord was my support" (Psalm 18: 6, 17-18—parenthetical material mine).*

Lord, You have been with me though this ordeal, and You will continue to sustain me and have the victory in Ben's life. In Jesus' name. Amen.

<u>Lessons Learned</u>: Wow! What an intense year. Ben went from being a captive to drugs to being set free! I was also captive to my own agenda. I thought I had figured out how my children's lives would unfold. God is setting me free from trying to be in control. I still am sad sometimes about Ben's life being screwed up so much, but I'm learning to be thankful he's alive and doing well. Many have died due to addictions. While there is life, there is still hope.

January 18th

Today I was putting away the Christmas decorations (I'd leave them up until spring if I had my way). I came upon two pictures of Ben—one as an infant and the other as a young child on Santa's lap. It made me want to cry...for a moment. He was so full of joy and eagerness. I had such hopes for him...but then I stopped dead in my tracks. I should be praising the Lord! He could still be in the grip of drugs, if it weren't for the Lord. Worse yet, he could be dead, like one of the neighbor's son-in-law. That made me wake up.

I continued to put decorations away, missing the days when the children were younger. As I put away three little bear magnets into their home for the rest of the year, I noticed all of them lost a different part of their ceramic body—an ear, a paw, or part of a candy cane. I thought the one that Ben claimed was the cutest, but now its foot was broken completely off from the many times Ben dropped it. Yet the bear still held a gift in his hand. The other two had minor missing pieces as compared to Ben's. As I looked at them, and yearned for their childhood, I got a flash of insight into my children, especially Ben.

His bear still held the present in his hands. His missing paw didn't impede that fact. Ben was still a gift, though maybe wounded or disabled a little like the bear. Then a deeper understanding dawned upon me. Ben still held unto the gift—of Jesus. What a comfort. I felt such a reassurance that Ben would not let go of that gift, no matter what happened in the past or in the future. He held on, just like the bear, with a smile on his face, and a lazy eye...just like Ben.

Dear Father,

Thank You for the flashes of insight into Your ways. Help me to hold on to this knowledge, and not let go. *"Now faith is the substance of things hoped for, the evidence of things not seen" (Hebrews 11:1).* You gave me faith during the crisis. Now help me to continue in faith, to continue to allow You to be *"my rock and my fortress, and my deliverer. My God, my strength, in who, I will trust" (Psalm 18:2).* I put my trust in You for Ben's future.

Suggestions: It was a long journey to get to this point, but when I look back I see God's hand in it. He is able to do *"Exceeding, abundantly above all that we ask or think" (Ephesians 3:20)*. God wants you to ask for what you need and have faith that He rewards you even when you falter. Don't think your faith is too small. *"If you have faith as a mustard seed, you will say to this mountain, 'Move from here to there' and it will move and nothing will be impossible for you" (Matthew 17: 20a)*. God moved mountains, in Ben's life and mine, but I spoke the Word and believed. Speak to your mountain, whatever it is, and trust God to move it. Wait patiently for Him to move. By the way, don't budge without Him!

End of January

This Thursday was a particularly touching graduation at Transformation Life Center. The music was very powerful now that they have a worship team together. I came in on the end of a lesson the pastor's wife was reviewing. The TLC boys and men were reading some of the points from the overhead in unison. It was touching to see them responding to the truth. The message the director brought had a different twist—how we can deceive ourselves into believing something that is blatantly not true. He used a personal illustration to drive the point home. It hit right between the eyes.

After graduation, I met some of the older men. They all had such wonderful things to say about Ben. It made me realize that he is becoming the person I envisioned, the man of

God I knew he could be. Who would have thought it would take a drug rehab, which was more like a Bible training school, to bring that out of him? I certainly wouldn't have chosen it to be that way. It wasn't God's perfect will for Ben to go through such hell, but in His goodness, the Lord worked out His will despite Ben's addiction, rebellion and stubbornness. God's ways are definitely not ours. Truly He is a great and mighty God, rich in mercy and abundant in loving kindness. I need to hold unto this truth.

Dear Father,

It's a beautiful sunny, though chilly morning, and Ben is coming home for a visit. Thank You for all the work you have done in him and will continue to do. I praise You for *"You have turned for me my mourning into dancing; You have put off my sackcloth and clothed me with gladness, To the end that my glory may sing praise to You and not be silent. O LORD my God, I will give thanks to You forever"* (Psalm 30: 10-12).

I will not be silent for You have granted my request for Ben to follow Your ways and be freed from the bondage of drugs and alcohol. I will continue to have a thankful heart and tell others about Your exceedingly excellent mercy and grace. May this journal help others in their journey to free their prodigal sons and daughters. In Jesus' name. Amen.

Epilogue

Ben went on to continue Phase two of the TLC Program and became a Resident Assistant. He became a dorm leader, RA, and solicited funds for the organization. He told everyone about the new freedom he's found in Jesus Christ. His faith has continued to grow, and God continued to heal him. His nervous habits, which were more pronounced the last few years of his life, diminished considerably, as well as his allergies. His natural compassion was properly funneled into healthy concern for others.

In April of 2009, he received news that he was accepted into the Radiology program at a local community college, which he applied to several years ago. He did very well and in 2010 was accepted into the Phi Beta Kappa Honor Society and was elected into the "Who's Who Among Students In American Universities and Colleges". He enjoyed his classes and practicum at the local hospital and loved what he was doing. Whenever opportunity knocked, he prayed with the patients who request it. In 2011, he graduated magna cum laude from the college.

Recently, Ben met a disabled man who was in a health care facility for over twenty years because of a car accident. The man was depressed and our son befriended him and started visiting him. Ben asked some of the men from TLC to write letters to the guy, and they gave him a Bible for Christmas. The man now

153

has hope for a future.

This is just one example of the how Ben reaches out to others. He also works with a disabled young man and takes him to church, to meetings and all over town. They have become buddies. Ben also attends several church meetings and reads his Bible faithfully. He is involved with a men's group, writes and sings Christian rap in various church venues, belongs to a college campus ministry and helps others in many different ways,

I can now agree with Ben that God has *"worked all things together for good for those he has called according to his purpose" (Romans 8:28).* As for myself, I have learned:

> "The words of the Lord are pure words,
> Like silver tried in a furnace of earth;
> Purified seven times.
> You shall keep them, O Lord,
> You shall preserve them from this generation forever" (Psalm 12:6).
>
> Praise Your name forever more!
>
> Praise God that He is the truth.
> He worked all things for good.
> And delivered my prodigal, safely home.

38978138R00088

Made in the USA
Lexington, KY
01 February 2015